MW01196040

Practical Applications of Ergonomics

ERGONOMICS

Humanizing the

Automated Office

Marilyn Joyce, President
The Joyce Institute
Seattle, Washington

with **Ulrika Wallersteiner, Ergonomist**
Ergo Systems Canada Inc.
Vancouver, British Columbia

Contributing Author
Marguerite Peterson
The Joyce Institute
Seattle, Washington

ISBN: 0-538-07643-7

1 2 3 4 5 6 7 8 K 5 4 3 2 1 0 9 8

Printed in the United States of America

COVER PHOTOS:
Top, © 1983 Roger Hill
Bottom, Courtesy STEELCASE INC.

G641
PUBLISHED BY
SOUTH-WESTERN PUBLISHING CO.
CINCINNATI   WEST CHICAGO, IL   CARROLLTON, TX   LIVERMORE, CA

TO THE STUDENT

Ergonomics is by definition an applied science that looks for practical solutions to issues and concerns existing in today's workplace. It focuses on the people side of office automation by concentrating on those aspects of ergonomics that affect employee performance, health, and well-being.

This *Practical Applications of Ergonomics* workbook contains a variety of projects designed to help you become actively involved with ergonomic concerns as they relate to real situations in automated offices. After completing the projects, you will be more aware of the many facets of ergonomics and the importance of ergonomics in the automated offices of today and tomorrow. This practical knowledge will help you understand better any office environment in which you may find yourself and will provide you with a basis to offer input into the planning, organizing, and managing of an automated office.

Many of the forms, survey instruments, and articles that you will use to complete your assignments will prove helpful to you in jobs you will hold in the future. Therefore, you will have an opportunity to build a valuable resource file as you complete the workbook activities.

TYPES OF PROJECTS

One or more projects are provided for each of the ten chapters in *Ergonomics: Humanizing the Automated Office*. While the activities vary a great deal, they generally fall into one of the following categories:

Field Research

Projects of this kind take you into the community where you will make observations and conduct surveys.

Interviews

Projects in this category take you into the community where you will interview individual workers using a prepared interview questionnaire. In many cases, you will be asked to contribute to the list of questions to be used.

Case Studies

Projects of this kind present realistic office situations briefly described. You are asked to assess each situation, make a decision, and support your recommendations.

Analyses

Projects in this category present you with data in various forms (questionnaires, notes from experts, charts, etc.). You frequently will be asked to analyze the data and make recommendations based upon your conclusions.

Readings

Reprints of magazine articles or position papers fall into this category. After reading each item, you will respond to questions about key points made.

The authors wish you well as you begin your study of ergonomics in the automated office. It is our hope that you will be able to apply the knowledge and experience you gain to any office environment in which you might find yourself. Ultimately, you may find yourself in a management position where you can "make a difference" and bring about the implementation of good ergonomic design in the workplace.

Marilyn Joyce
Ulrika Wallersteiner
Marguerite Peterson

CONTENTS

CHAPTER 7   THE ENVIRONMENT: SPACE DESIGN

CHAPTER 8   THE ENVIRONMENT: LIGHTING, ACOUSTICS, THERMAL COMFORT, AND AIR QUALITY

CHAPTER 9   TRAINING

CHAPTER 10   ERGONOMICS: TODAY AND TOMORROW

Everyday Ergonomics

There are situations at school, at work, and in your leisure activities where you experience characteristics of good and poor ergonomics. While poor ergonomics can lead to frustration, danger, discomfort, and poor performance, good ergonomics in the design of the environment, tools, and tasks can increase comfort and enhance performance.

PROJECT 1 ERGONOMIC AWARENESS

Objective: to determine how widespread is the awareness of ergonomics.

Instructions

1. Find and make copies, if possible, of magazine and newspaper advertisements that make reference to ergonomics.

2. Go to your school or local library and identify two books and three magazine articles that include "ergonomics" as part of the title. Give complete references. (For example, Wilbert O. Galitz, *The Office Environment: Automation's Impact on Tomorrow's Workplace:* Willow Grove, Administrative Management Society, 1984.)

   Book _____

   _____

   Book _____

   _____

   Magazine article _____

   _____

   Magazine article _____

   _____

   Magazine article _____

   _____

3. Interview four people (relatives, friends, neighbors) to determine their knowledge of ergonomics and ergonomic principles. Use the questionnaires provided on pages 3 and 5.

4. Write a summary of your conclusions after completing steps 1, 2, and 3 above. Title the summary "Ergonomic Awareness." Discuss how aware you think people are of the term ergonomics and of ergonomic principles both in their personal lives and in their work lives.

ERGONOMICS AWARENESS QUESTIONNAIRE

1. Are you familiar with the term ERGONOMICS?   Yes____ No____

2. With what do you associate the term ERGONOMICS? _____
_____

3. Do you think ergonomics relates to the following areas?

	Yes	No	Don't Know
space planning	___	___	___
lighting	___	___	___
selection of office furniture, chairs, and accessories	___	___	___
equipment selection	___	___	___
worker training	___	___	___
training supervisors of workers	___	___	___
software design	___	___	___
task analysis and job design	___	___	___

4. Actually, ergonomics is "the science that studies people's performance and well-being in the workplace." The purpose of ergonomics is to improve the health, well-being, and performance of workers by making the jobs, equipment, and environment compatible with people's characteristics and needs. On a scale of 1 to 10, with 10 meaning extremely important, how would you evaluate the importance of ergonomic implementation for an organization? _____

_____   _____
Name   Position

ERGONOMICS AWARENESS QUESTIONNAIRE

1. Are you familiar with the term ERGONOMICS?   Yes____ No____

2. With what do you associate the term ERGONOMICS? _____
_____

3. Do you think ergonomics relates to the following areas?

	Yes	No	Don't Know
space planning	___	___	___
lighting	___	___	___
selection of office furniture, chairs, and accessories	___	___	___
equipment selection	___	___	___
worker training	___	___	___
training supervisors of workers	___	___	___
software design	___	___	___
task analysis and job design	___	___	___

4. Actually, ergonomics is "the science that studies people's performance and well-being in the workplace." The purpose of ergonomics is to improve the health, well-being, and performance of workers by making the jobs, equipment, and environment compatible with people's characteristics and needs. On a scale of 1 to 10, with 10 meaning extremely important, how would you evaluate the importance of ergonomic implementation for an organization? _____

_____   _____
Name   Position

ERGONOMICS AWARENESS QUESTIONNAIRE

1. Are you familiar with the term ERGONOMICS?   Yes____ No____

2. With what do you associate the term ERGONOMICS? _____
_____

3. Do you think ergonomics relates to the following areas?

	Yes	No	Don't Know
space planning	___	___	___
lighting	___	___	___
selection of office furniture, chairs, and accessories	___	___	___
equipment selection	___	___	___
worker training	___	___	___
training supervisors of workers	___	___	___
software design	___	___	___
task analysis and job design	___	___	___

4. Actually, ergonomics is "the science that studies people's performance and well-being in the workplace." The purpose of ergonomics is to improve the health, well-being, and performance of workers by making the jobs, equipment, and environment compatible with people's characteristics and needs. On a scale of 1 to 10, with 10 meaning extremely important, how would you evaluate the importance of ergonomic implementation for an organization? _____

_____   _____
Name   Position

- -

ERGONOMICS AWARENESS QUESTIONNAIRE

1. Are you familiar with the term ERGONOMICS?   Yes____ No____

2. With what do you associate the term ERGONOMICS? _____
_____

3. Do you think ergonomics relates to the following areas?

	Yes	No	Don't Know
space planning	___	___	___
lighting	___	___	___
selection of office furniture, chairs, and accessories	___	___	___
equipment selection	___	___	___
worker training	___	___	___
training supervisors of workers	___	___	___
software design	___	___	___
task analysis and job design	___	___	___

4. Actually, ergonomics is "the science that studies people's performance and well-being in the workplace." The purpose of ergonomics is to improve the health, well-being, and performance of workers by making the jobs, equipment, and environment compatible with people's characteristics and needs. On a scale of 1 to 10, with 10 meaning extremely important, how would you evaluate the importance of ergonomic implementation for an organization? _____

_____   _____
Name   Position

Ergonomics and Office Automation

One of management's major responsibilities in today's automated office is to ensure that the investment in technology is maximized. Awareness of the role ergonomics plays in providing for employees' physical and psychological needs is essential. When the Six Key Elements — job design, equipment, software design, workstation design, environment, and training are considered as part of the overall implementation, you find more productive computer usage and higher job satisfaction. When any of the Key Elements are ignored, individual performance and well-being are diminished and organizational efficiency threatened.

PROJECT 1 ERGONOMICS, TODAY AND TOMORROW

Objective: to broaden your perception of the impact of ergonomics in the workplace.

Instructions

1. Read the executive summary on pages 9–12 titled "The Office Environment, Automation's Impact on Tomorrow's Workplace."

2. Answer the questions on page 12.

PROJECT 2 HEALTH/COMFORT SURVEY

Objective: to determine if office workers using computers report common discomforts experienced by other VDT users.

Instructions

1. Use the survey forms on pages 13, 15, and 17 to survey six office workers who use computers or word processors. Determine to what degree (if any) the workers suffer from common discomforts reported by VDT users.

2. Tally the results of your survey by transferring the information from the survey forms to the Health/Comfort Survey Results form on page 19. Calculate the totals for those who did/did not experience: (a) psychological/emotional problems, (b) eye problems, and (c) musculoskeletal problems.

THE OFFICE ENVIRONMENT
Automation's Impact on Tomorrow's Workplace

The second of a four-part study on "Managing the Office — 1990 and Beyond," sponsored in part by a grant from the Olsten Corporation

Wilbert O. Galitz
President - Galitz, Inc.
St. Charles, Illinois

Executive Summary

In recent years, with human productivity waning and technology steadily infiltrating the office, the importance of the office environment and the role it plays in human productivity is becoming much more apparent. Systems that fail to achieve their objectives, health hazard concerns, and results of research studies are providing dramatic evidence that the office environment fulfills a key role in the successful implementation of the new technologies beginning to shape what is called the office of the future.

This monograph examines the changing office environment and the impact automation is having on tomorrow's workplace. Its goal is to aid managers in planning tomorrow's office so that the potential benefits of automation may actually be achieved. This work summarizes research studies on the effects of environmental factors on office workers. Based on these findings, it pinpoints major concerns and specifically defines environmental ingredients of tomorrow's office, including such elements as lighting, acoustics, climate, workstations, and office layout.

The following presents highlights of this monograph.

The video display terminal (VDT) and the VDT workstation play a role in reported discomforts. A portion of the reported problems appear to be real. The physiology of the human eye and body is not always compatible with the way VDTs are manufactured and installed. VDTs have been manufactured with display characteristics that can fatigue the human eye, and with components arranged to force their users to assume uncomfortable, constrained, and fatiguing postures. VDTs have also been installed in offices in a haphazard way with little thought to good viewing and operating conditions.

Use of VDTs need not be physically fatiguing, however, as evidenced by the people and studies that report no problems. A properly designed VDT and good work environment, while probably not totally devoid of discomforts in today's state of the art, can be made much more comfortable to work with than is commonly the case. Solutions to problems, however, cannot be accomplished by independently addressing the equipment and environment.

Job content also plays a significant role in reported discomforts. Reports of physical ailments can be influenced by the content of the job being performed. Some studies have found higher incidences of physical complaints among clerical users than among professional users of VDTs. The job content of professional users included flexibility in accomplishing goals, control over tasks, utilization of experience and education, and satisfaction and pride in an end product, the kinds of qualities missing from many clerical tasks.

Thus the impact of the job, and the design of the system, have a much larger impact on satisfaction and work stress than many early researchers suspected. The psychosocial needs can overshadow physical needs in a variety of human experiences.

Length of working time plays a role in reported discomforts. It has been found that as the amount of working time at various VDT jobs increases, so does the percentage of workers expressing psychosocial problems. Shorter time periods at VDTs provide opportunities to rest muscles and permit a greater variety in movements and tasks. Studies have yet to be made on optimum time periods but observation indicates that two hours or less a day at the VDT relieves many of the physical problems.

Individual differences play a role in susceptibility to discomfort. No two people are alike. Human physiques, traits, and sensitivities are distributed along the normal distribution curve. The viewing angle of a VDT located in a standardized position may be proper for one person but not for another. One person may perceive display flicker while a second does not in an identical viewing condition. Solutions must consider individual differences; variable opinions and responses are the norm.

Possible adverse health effects associated with VDT use include reports of unusually high numbers of miscarriages, birth defects and eye cataracts. In reaction to these concerns, a number of studies of the radiation emission qualities of VDTs have been performed by a variety of governmental and nongovernmental organizations around the world. Based on the results of these studies, and the findings of their own study, the authors of the Environmental Health Directorate report (1983) conclude: "There is no reason for any person, male or female, young or old, pregnant or not, to be concerned about radiation health effects from VDTs." Statements like this, however, will probably not end the controversy. We must continue to search for answers that assure everyone that the accelerating use of VDTs is a safe path to follow.

We need to continue the research needed to establish cause and effects while at the same time assuring that VDTs are used properly within the limits of today's knowledge.

Workstation design has become more complex due to the incorporation of the VDT. The VDT has caused awkward terminal operating positions, lost workspace, and inefficient workspace organization. To counter these, and provide an efficient working environment, a host of new considerations must be addressed. Workstation design must incorporate the demands of technology, the tasks to be performed, and various human needs. Providing for human needs involves consideration of both biological needs (body dimensions, sensory, and ambient), and psychological needs (intellectual, social, motivational, and aesthetic). Recognizing the increasingly complex and individualized nature of workstation design, the office furniture industry is moving to a systems approach, involving such elements as task/ambient lighting, component furniture systems, modular storage, and easily adjustable components. Furthermore, the dramatic increase in the variety of elements and services that support a VDT (such as lighting, telephone and data communication cables) will ultimately make workstations more built-in and fixed in location.

Attention to the lighting needs of workers at office systems is now extremely important. Serious attention to lighting is warranted by the impact it can have on worker productivity and health. The increasing complexity of office lighting also requires greater involvement of lighting consultants, since proceeding in ignorance may cause more harm than good. In sum, task/ambient lighting can help solve office lighting problems posed by VDTs. Extreme care must be taken, however, to provide a quality solution. It is important to avoid shadows as well as glare, bright and dim spots, poorly directed light, and similar conditions.

An office layout should optimize the flow of work among various departments and people. It should also minimize movement and sound distractions caused by people going about their activities. The following principles should determine office layouts.
• Keep people close to those with whom they must frequently communicate.
• Keep files and other references close to the people who use them.
• Keep people who have many outside visitors close to the work area entrance.
• Common destinations (toilets, elevators, photocopy machines, and so on) should be close together and accessible by direct routes.
• Workstations should be away from sources of intermittent sounds and areas of frequent conversations.

Toward the Year 2000

Human factors and ergonomic considerations will achieve ever-increasing importance in future environmental design as awareness of their contribution to greater human productivity grows. That this is happening is evidenced by the fact that four of the top five critical human resource problems identified in the first monograph in this series are people-related and can be addressed through application of human factors/ergonomic design principles. That this is happening is also evidenced by the contents of this monograph.

Information. Previously scattered information will be electronically consolidated, thereby reducing the clutter of the workstation. Information will be more accessible to all. Paper will not entirely disappear, however.

Technology. Miniaturization of technology will continue. The bulky cathode ray tube (CRT) will gradually be replaced by flat-panel displays offering compactness, increased mobility, and the capability of being built into the workstation. Advances in display support electronics will yield improved resolution, color, split-screen capabilities and three-dimensional perspectives. Larger displays will also be available, permitting the presentation of more information at one time.

The typewriter-type keyboard will remain a primary human-computer interface mechanism, but touch-panel displays and pointers such as the mouse and trackballs will have widespread use. Voice recognition and synthesis will be viable in a variety of applications. Workstations will be more built-in and fixed in location. The next major restructuring of the workstation will occur as the components of the computer interface system are included within the working surfaces themselves. Terminals will cease to be instruments supported by a surface, but will become part of the work surface. In some ways the workstation may become one large terminal.

Another technology on the horizon will soon have a large impact on workstation design—talking computers. Voice communications between people and systems will usher in a whole new era of acoustical concerns and solutions as the office din increases while workstation size decreases as a result of more costly office space. The creative worker, while being freed from the mechanics of interfacing with a keyboard, will be exposed to the distractions caused by an escalating major noise source in the office, the human voice.

Ultimately, an effective workstation design is going to require even closer cooperation among all interested parties—furniture manufacturers, terminal manufacturers, facility managers, and computer-users. Those who are not yet talking to each other had better start quickly.

The workstation of tomorrow will be smaller. Electronic information consolidation will eliminate the need for large areas to store information on paper and the materials needed for paper handling. At the same time, however, greater visual and auditory privacy will be needed. Noise created by equipment and voice computer interaction will create severe acoustical problems. Display terminals and other technologies will be incorporated within the workstation itself. The surface of the desk and workstation walls will become control and viewing surfaces. The chair may also contain fingertip controls. The office workstation and the airplane cockpit may bear some resemblance to each other.

Comfort in working will be achieved through intelligent chairs and desks. Desk heights and angles will be modified through the simple touch of a button. Desired configurations will be remembered by the desk's electronics and changed as the needs of a person change.

The chair may actually configure itself to its occupant through analysis of weight distribution.

Office buildings as we know them today will continue to operate. A reduction in paper and paper filing requirements, and more people working at home or in satellite offices, will diminish space requirements, however. Offices and conference rooms will also still exist. Electronic meetings are a poor substitute for a variety of communications requiring interpersonal interaction. These will best be addressed by people facing people.

Tomorrow's office will provide a computer utility akin to that provided by the electric and telephone companies. A variety of computing services will be available as easily as turning on a light switch.

The technology of tomorrow raises some critical environmental issues that must be addressed. Each will have a significant impact on the well-being of the office worker and the organization. These issues pertain to noise, electronic social isolation, and health.

Noise. As human-computer interaction methods change, and voice communication assumes a greater role in the dialogue, a new dimension will be added to the office din. Talking people and talking computers will be an even greater source of distraction. An office acoustics program will be necessary to keep sound and noise levels within a range that is comfortable for performing human office activities. Those levels should eliminate distractions, allow good hearing and provide speech privacy.

Tomorrow's office must provide the proper social environment as well. As we direct more and more of our attention to the computer and structure our workstations around it, the office design must still foster and encourage the human-to-human interactions so vital to us all. The environment must provide the degree of privacy demanded by the new technologies while at the same time not inhibit the necessary face-to-face communications of people with other people.

Tomorrow's jobs must not be made too comfortable. Organization of the items comprising the workstation and the job themselves must have within them the requirement for a certain degree of physical movement. The challenge will be to stay on the right side of the line separating healthy diversity from fatigue. Workstation component adjustability will be a key element in achieving this objective. Being able to easily assume a variety of different working postures during the day will provide needed exercise for a range of muscles. Health clubs or exercise rooms may also become integral parts of the office. The coffee break, now used to mentally and physically recharge fatigued minds and bodies, may be supplemented by the exercise break to replenish stiff and rigid bodies.

Lastly, legislation may impose an unnecessary financial burden on the occasional users of VDTs. Occasional users are not subjected to all the problems described here; to impose solutions to non-problems is not cost effective. Furthermore, state or Federally mandated requirements necessitate monitoring mechanisms to assure company compliance with the law. This results in tax dollars being spent for solutions of dubious long-term value to companies and society.

Psychosocial problems and the physical ailments associated with posture and vision cannot really be neatly divided into separate categories. Nor can the effects of the hardware, the system, the environment, and an organization's management. The worker, too, must be looked upon not just as one but as many with a variety of needs, interests, attitudes and susceptibilities.

A tangible benefit of increased attention to the environment will be increased productivity. Intangible benefits include decreased absenteeism, improved job satisfaction and morale, and lowered workers' compensation claims and costs. Humanizing the workplace can also serve as a proactive response to the charges by interest groups and organized labor about the health and safety of working with VDTs.

We must not lose sight of the fact, however, that the road to successful office system implementation requires complete harmony of the worker, the organization, and the technology. The product of our efforts must result in a condition where jobs, computer systems, equipment, the work environment, and motivations and psychological needs of the workers are properly woven into a whole office fabric. Then the process of change must be carefully managed. The results of our efforts will be no stronger than the weakest thread.

Galitz, Wilbert O. *The Office Environment: Automation's Impact on Tomorrow's Workplace.* (Trevose, PA: Administrative Management Society Foundation, 1984), pg. 5–11. Reprinted with permission.

1. What are some of the key influences on worker discomfort?
_____
_____

2. What factors do professional users often find in their jobs which tend to decrease discomfort?
_____
_____

3. What is the conclusion of the Environmental Health Directorate report regarding the adverse effects of radiation emission from VDTs?
_____
_____

4. Why is workstation design so complex since the incorporation of the VDT?
_____
_____

5. What are some general principles which should determine office layout?
_____
_____

6. What are some of the technological advances predicted as we move toward the year 2000?
_____
_____

7. What are some critical environmental issues that could result from these advancements?
_____
_____

HEALTH/COMFORT SURVEY

1. Have you ever experienced any of the following during your work? Indicate the degree by placing a checkmark in the appropriate box: F-Frequently (once a week or more); O-Occasionally (approximately twice a month); S-Sometimes (isolated incidents); N-Never (absolutely no occasions).

	F	O	S	N
Fatigue				
Headache				
Irritated eyes				
Eyestrain				

	F	O	S	N
Back pain				
Painful/stiff neck or shoulders				
Painful/stiff arms and legs				
Stiff/sore wrists or hands				

2. How often do you take a break away from your work area? _____

3. How often do you go outdoors during a typical workday? _____

4. How much coffee/tea with caffeine do you drink a day? _____

5. What type of physical activity for recreation do you do? _____

_____ _____
Name   Occupation

- -

HEALTH/COMFORT SURVEY

1. Have you ever experienced any of the following during your work? Indicate the degree by placing a checkmark in the appropriate box: F-Frequently (once a week or more); O-Occasionally (approximately twice a month); S-Sometimes (isolated incidents); N-Never (absolutely no occasions).

	F	O	S	N
Fatigue				
Headache				
Irritated eyes				
Eyestrain				

	F	O	S	N
Back pain				
Painful/stiff neck or shoulders				
Painful/stiff arms and legs				
Stiff/sore wrists or hands				

2. How often do you take a break away from your work area? _____

3. How often do you go outdoors during a typical workday? _____

4. How much coffee/tea with caffeine do you drink a day? _____

5. What type of physical activity for recreation do you do? _____

_____ _____
Name   Occupation

HEALTH/COMFORT SURVEY

1. Have you ever experienced any of the following during your work? Indicate the degree by placing a checkmark in the appropriate box: F-Frequently (once a week or more); O-Occasionally (approximately twice a month); S-Sometimes (isolated incidents); N-Never (absolutely no occasions).

	F	O	S	N
Fatigue				
Headache				
Irritated eyes				
Eyestrain				

	F	O	S	N
Back pain				
Painful/stiff neck or shoulders				
Painful/stiff arms and legs				
Stiff/sore wrists or hands				

2. How often do you take a break away from your work area? _____

3. How often do you go outdoors during a typical workday? _____

4. How much coffee/tea with caffeine do you drink a day? _____

5. What type of physical activity for recreation do you do? _____

_____   _____
Name   Occupation

- -

HEALTH/COMFORT SURVEY

1. Have you ever experienced any of the following during your work? Indicate the degree by placing a checkmark in the appropriate box: F-Frequently (once a week or more); O-Occasionally (approximately twice a month); S-Sometimes (isolated incidents); N-Never (absolutely no occasions).

	F	O	S	N
Fatigue				
Headache				
Irritated eyes				
Eyestrain				

	F	O	S	N
Back pain				
Painful/stiff neck or shoulders				
Painful/stiff arms and legs				
Stiff/sore wrists or hands				

2. How often do you take a break away from your work area? _____

3. How often do you go outdoors during a typical workday? _____

4. How much coffee/tea with caffeine do you drink a day? _____

5. What type of physical activity for recreation do you do? _____

_____   _____
Name   Occupation

HEALTH/COMFORT SURVEY

1. Have you ever experienced any of the following during your work? Indicate the degree by placing a checkmark in the appropriate box: F-Frequently (once a week or more); O-Occasionally (approximately twice a month); S-Sometimes (isolated incidents); N-Never (absolutely no occasions).

	F	O	S	N
Fatigue				
Headache				
Irritated eyes				
Eyestrain				

	F	O	S	N
Back pain				
Painful/stiff neck or shoulders				
Painful/stiff arms and legs				
Stiff/sore wrists or hands				

2. How often do you take a break away from your work area?_____

3. How often do you go outdoors during a typical workday?_____

4. How much coffee/tea with caffeine do you drink a day?_____

5. What type of physical activity for recreation do you do?_____

_____   _____
Name   Occupation

- -

HEALTH/COMFORT SURVEY

1. Have you ever experienced any of the following during your work? Indicate the degree by placing a checkmark in the appropriate box: F-Frequently (once a week or more); O-Occasionally (approximately twice a month); S-Sometimes (isolated incidents); N-Never (absolutely no occasions).

	F	O	S	N
Fatigue				
Headache				
Irritated eyes				
Eyestrain				

	F	O	S	N
Back pain				
Painful/stiff neck or shoulders				
Painful/stiff arms and legs				
Stiff/sore wrists or hands				

2. How often do you take a break away from your work area?_____

3. How often do you go outdoors during a typical workday?_____

4. How much coffee/tea with caffeine do you drink a day?_____

5. What type of physical activity for recreation do you do?_____

_____   _____
Name   Occupation

HEALTH/COMFORT SURVEY RESULTS

SYMPTOMS	Frequently	Occasionally	Sometimes	Never	Totals
PSYCHOLOGICAL/EMOTIONAL EFFECTS OF VDT WORK Fatigue					
Headache					
Total workers experiencing psychological/emotional problems					(a) _____
EFFECTS OF VDT WORK ON THE EYES Irritated eyes					
Eyestrain					
Total workers experiencing eye problems					(b) _____
MUSCULOSKELETAL EFFECTS OF VDT WORK Back pain					
Painful neck/shoulders					
Painful arms/legs					
Stiff/sore wrists or hands					
Total workers experiencing musculoskeletal problems					(c) _____

Job Design

> To create a productive and satisfying job environment in the automated workplace, managers and supervisors must frequently evaluate how jobs are modified by the changing technology. Any technological improvement (software or hardware) will most likely impact the way a job is done and/or the overall "job design." Periodic job task analyses that pinpoint duties and responsibilities and preferences help to design ergonomic jobs consisting of the five elements of Variety, Identity/Importance, Autonomy/Control, Feedback/Recognition, and an opportunity for personal growth.

PROJECT 1 HOW ERGONOMIC IS YOUR JOB?

Objective: to help you understand how a job is affected by the five ergonomic elements of good job design.

Instructions

1. Interview two people who work in offices. You will use the questionnaires on pages 23 and 25 so be sure to read over the questions carefully before you conduct the interviews. Also, you are encouraged to ask a question of your choosing. (Write your questions on the lines provided on the questionnaire.)

2. Conduct the two interviews. Be sure to fully inform your interviewees of the purpose of your questions. Record their responses on the appropriate lines of the questionnaire.

PROJECT 2 PREPARING FOR AN INTERVIEW

Objective: to demonstrate the importance of ergonomic principles from the job applicant's perspective.

Instructions

1. Select one of the following jobs (or select one of your own choice) and assume that you are interviewing for that position. Compose at least four questions that you will ask at the interview.

   word processor - lawyer's office
   billing/inventory clerk - general office of a university
   accounting - large accounting firm
   customer service representative - utilities company

   Question 1 _____

   _____

   _____

   _____

(continued)

Question 2 _____

_____

_____

Question 3 _____

_____

_____

Question 4 _____

_____

_____

PROJECT 3 ANALYZING A JOB

Objective: to learn to analyze information from questionnaires/forms and use problem-solving approaches.

Instructions

Review the completed job design evaluation form (page 27) completed by Howard Avery, secretary/receptionist.

1. Based on what you learned from the job design evaluation and what you learned about job design in Chapter 3, what general recommendations would you make to his supervisors?

_____

_____

_____

_____

_____

_____

2. What questions might you ask Howard to further discover how he thinks his job could be improved?

Question 1 _____

_____

_____

Question 2 _____

_____

Question 3 _____

_____

_____

ERGONOMIC JOB QUESTIONNAIRE

Name of person interviewed _____

Company name _____

Address _____

Job title_____

Major areas of responsibility_____

_____

_____

_____

_____

Variety

a. Does your job include a variety of tasks or the repetition of one task?

_____

_____

b. Does your job involve

    Too many tasks?____ Not enough tasks?____

    Just the right number?____

c. (Question of your choice)

    Does your job _____ ?

    _____

    _____

    _____

Identity/Importance

a. How does your work fit into the larger operation of the company?

_____

_____

b. Do you feel that your work is

    Highly essential?____ Somewhat essential?____

    Not essential?____

c. (Question of your choice)

    Does your job _____ ?

    _____

    _____

    _____

(continued)

Feedback/Recognition

a. How do you know if your employer is happy with your work?

_____

_____

b. If you are evaluated, how often does this evaluation occur?

Once a year?____ Once a month?____

Other?____

c. (Question of your choice)

Does your job _____ ?

_____

_____

_____

Personal Growth

a. What experiences are you getting from this job that will help you in future positions with your current employer or with a new employer?

_____

_____

b. What training opportunities are available?

On-site classes?____ College courses?____

Other?____

c. (Question of your choice)

Does your job_____ ?

_____

_____

_____

Autonomy/Control

a. Do you make decisions regarding *how* you do your job?_____

_____

_____

_____

b. How are priorities and time frames established?

You decide____ Someone else decides____

You and someone else decide____

c. (Question of your choice)

Does your job_____ ?

_____

_____

_____

ERGONOMIC JOB QUESTIONNAIRE

Name of person interviewed _____

Company name _____

Address _____

Job title_____

Major areas of responsibility_____

_____

_____

_____

_____

Variety

a.   Does your job include a variety of tasks or the repetition of one task?

_____

_____

b.   Does your job involve

        Too many tasks?____   Not enough tasks?____

        Just the right number?____

c.   (Question of your choice)

        Does your job _____ ?

_____

_____

_____

Identity/Importance

a.   How does your work fit into the larger operation of the company?

_____

_____

b.   Do you feel that your work is

        Highly essential?____   Somewhat essential?____

        Not essential?____

c.   (Question of your choice)

        Does your job _____ ?

_____

_____

_____

(continued)

Feedback/Recognition

a. How do you know if your employer is happy with your work?

_____

_____

b. If you are evaluated, how often does this evaluation occur?

Once a year?____ Once a month?____

Other?____

c. (Question of your choice)

Does your job _____?

_____

_____

_____

Personal Growth

a. What experiences are you getting from this job that will help you in future positions with your current employer or with a new employer?

_____

_____

b. What training opportunities are available?

On-site classes?____ College courses?____

Other?____

c. (Question of your choice)

Does your job_____?

_____

_____

_____

Autonomy/Control

a. Do you make decisions regarding *how* you do your job?_____

_____

_____

_____

b. How are priorities and time frames established?

You decide____ Someone else decides____

You and someone else decide____

c. (Question of your choice)

Does your job_____?

_____

_____

_____

JOB DESIGN EVALUATION

JOB ANALYSIS QUESTIONNAIRE PART 3

Please answer the following questions about your job. (On the questions which include categories, please check only one item.)

Name: *Howard Avery*

Job Title: *Secretary/Receptionist*

1. Are you satisfied with your job?   Yes   (Somewhat)   No

2. Are there aspects of your job that could be improved?

    (Yes)   No   Don't know

3. How many different types of tasks do you do?   *5-8*

4. Do you feel
   - Overworked   ✓
   - Underworked   _____
   - In control   _____

5. Does your job consist of
   - Completion of many steps of a process   ✓
   - Doing only one or two steps of a process   _____
   - Seeing a project through from the
     beginning to the end   _____

6. Who determines the order and amount of time
   you spend on each task in a day?
   - You   _____
   - You along with your manager/supervisor   ✓
   - Your manager/supervisor   _____
   - The computer/software   _____

7. How is your work evaluated?
   - Formal evaluation   _____
   - Comments from supervisor   _____
   - Formal evaluation and comments
     from supervisor   ✓
   - Feedback from the computer   _____

8. How often do you get feedback?
   - Once a year   ✓
   - Once a month   _____
   - Weekly   _____
   - Daily   _____
   - On a project by project basis   _____
   - Sporadically   _____

9. Do you ever have the opportunity to participate
   in training classes or go to conferences?   Yes   (No)

10. Are you made aware of promotion opportunities?   Yes   (No)

The Equipment

One of the most important decisions management and staff make when an office is automated is the specific equipment to be purchased. Technological development has produced a vast array of VDT monitors, keyboard styles, and printer capabilities. Experts in the field of ergonomics stress the importance of training workers to use the equipment properly. Also of importance is the selection of equipment features that are ergonomically sound and designed for the intended purpose. Ergonomically designed equipment adheres to certain guidelines that enable the user to operate it safely and efficiently.

PROJECT 1 FIELD RESEARCH (MONITOR COMPARISONS)

Objective: to assess the ergonomic soundness of different computer monitors.

Instructions

1. VDT screens vary a great deal in the areas of legibility, brightness, color, and structural configuration. Visit a computer store or an office where a variety of computers can be found.

2. Be familiar with each of three different screens by sitting and experimenting with all adjustable features. Use the monitor comparison sheet on page 31 to help you assess the ergonomic soundness of the three monitors you are evaluating. Rate each screen on a scale of 1–5 (with 5 being the best or highest rating) for each factor listed. Then answer the question at the bottom of the comparison sheet.

PROJECT 2 EXPERIMENTING WITH PINK AFTER-IMAGES

Objective: to develop understanding of the common phenomenon of after-image.

Instructions

1. Computer operators sometimes report seeing pink after-images after working with a green display. Locate a computer with a green display (it might, for example, be a black background with green images). Spend 10 minutes looking at the display. Then look at a white or off-white wall or piece of paper. (a) Do you see pink images? _____ (b) If yes, how long did the pink effect last?

    _____

2. Read the article on page 30 for a scientific explanation of the after-image phenomenon. Then summarize in your own words the answer to the question: "What causes pink after-images?"

WHAT CAUSES RED OR PINK AFTER-IMAGES?

Mixing red and yellow light together (for example, by shining light from two slide projectors—one equipped with a yellow filter and one with red—onto a white screen) will create an orange image. Likewise, mixing yellow and green light will produce yellowish-green. In other words, looking at the color spectrum, a color can be created by mixing light from color around it.

But mixing light from more widely separated colors in the spectrum produces only gray. Examples are yellow and blue, and red and green. Colors which create gray when their light is added together are called complements. Red is the complement of green and vice versa.

Looking to a white or gray surface after staring at any color for a period is likely to result in the momentary perception of its complement. Thus, VDT operators commonly see pink for a brief period after a long vigil of working at a display with green characters.

The cause of the pink after-image is adaptation and thus temporary loss of sensitivity of the red-green sensors of the visual system to green. Sensitivity to red is unaffected. Therefore, when the gaze is shifted away from the green field, there is a somewhat greater propensity to see red until green sensitivity is restored.

Though sometimes annoying, after-images are not harmful, and usually last only a few moments. Some operators report that they control pink after-images by affixing a border of red construction paper to their displays. Switching to a display with a different color is another solution, but complementary after-images are always a possibility with any color dominating the visual field.

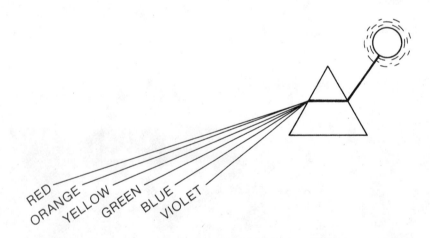

COLOR SPECTRUM

Steven L. Sauter, John Chapman, and Sheri J. Knutson. *Improving VDT Work — Causes and Control of Health Concerns in VDT Use.* Prepared for the Department of Administration, State of Wisconsin. (Department of Preventive Medicine, University of Wisconsin, 1985), p. 56. Used with permission.

MONITOR COMPARISON

Factors to Investigate	SCREENS		
	Screen 1	Screen 2	Screen 3
	Brand/Model	Brand/Model	Brand/Model
LEGIBILITY Character test			
SCREEN BRIGHTNESS Adjustability for contrast			
SCREEN COLOR Positive/Negative contrast			
STRUCTURAL CONFIGURATION Adjustable placement features: screen tilt			
TOTALS			

If you were choosing a monitor to work with, which one would you choose and why?

_____

_____

_____

_____

_____

PROJECT 3 FAST LANE OR SLOW LANE?

Objective: to realize the effect of ergonomic design on a worker's efficiency.

Instructions

1. There are three basic keyboards: the QWERTY, the Dvorak, and the alphabetic. A discussion of each keyboard follows. Read each discussion and give attention to the arrangement of the keys on each keyboard.

2. Answer the questions about keyboards on pages 35 and 36.

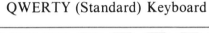

QWERTY (Standard) Keyboard

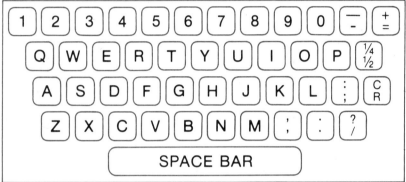

The most common keyboard today, called the QWERTY or standard keyboard, was designed by Christopher Sholes. His keyboard was named after the six alphabetic letters in the top alphabetic row of the keyboard. Although Sholes is referred to as the "father of the typewriter," he was in fact the fifty-second man to invent a typewriter. He did, however, invent the first *practical* typewriter. Earlier keyboards had the letters (which sat atop little spokes that were raised to the paper when a particular key was struck) arranged in such a way that keys frequently struck consecutively to form common words were placed closed together. This caused frequent jamming of the keys in the key basket with the result that using earlier typewriters was as slow, or slower, than writing with a pen. Sholes reordered the letters to avoid the key clash, thereby increasing typing speed as well as the efficiency of the typewriter and the typist.

For example, he distributed the most common letters (E, T, O, A, N, and I) over the entire keyboard and placed the letters that were part of frequent combinations (for example, de and fr) so they had to be struck with the same finger. A typist using the keyboard uses the left hand 57 percent of the time.

(continued)

DVORAK (Simplified) Keyboard

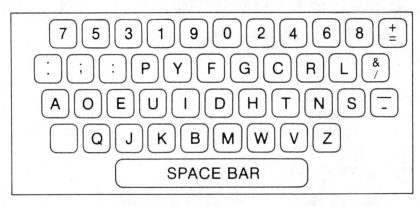

The Dvorak keyboard was invented by August Dvorak, who received two Carnegie Corporation grants in 1933 and 1934. He felt his new keyboard design improved on the QWERTY keyboard in arrangement, productivity, and style. In order to achieve his primary goal of speed, he placed all five vowels and the five most common consonants (D, H, Y, N, and S) on the home row. A typist using the Dvorak keyboard can type approximately 4,000 common English words with just these letters, as opposed to only 150 common words on the QWERTY. Seventy percent of all general typing can be done on the home row of the Dvorak keyboard. Also, the right hand is used 56 percent of the time. Other important keys, such as the comma, are placed above (rather than below) the home row because it is easier for a typist to move his or her fingers up than down. Reportedly, learning time is significantly reduced on the Dvorak keyboard. Some keyboarding equipment today comes with a choice of either the QWERTY or the Dvorak keyboard.

ALPHABETIC Keyboard

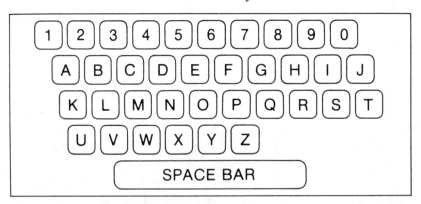

The alphabetic layout is chiefly used in non-typing situations for non-typists. You may see this type of keyboard on children's computers where the reinforcement of learning alphabetic order is a side benefit of educational games. They are also frequently used for automatic bank teller machines and for other customer service transactions where there can be no presumption that the user has typing expertise or knowledge of the QWERTY layout.

Sources: Bruce Bliven, Jr., *The Wonderful Writing Machine* (New York: Random House, 1954) and William Hoffer, "The Dvorak Keyboard: Is It Your Type?" *Nation's Business* (August 1985), pp. 38-40. See also Stephanie K. Walter, "The Dvorak Keyboard: A Better Mousetrap?" *Management Technology* (February 1984), p. 76.

KEYBOARDS

1. Compare the QWERTY and Dvorak keyboards by completing the following:

   a. List several common combinations that are hit with the same finger on the QWERTY keyboard (e.g. "ol").

   _____ _____ _____

   b. List 20 common words that can be produced from letters on the home row on the Dvorak keyboard. Then, try to create a list using the QWERTY home row. Can you do it?

   Dvorak

   _____ _____ _____
   _____ _____ _____
   _____ _____ _____
   _____ _____ _____
   _____ _____ _____
   _____ _____ _____
   _____   _____

   QWERTY

   _____ _____ _____
   _____ _____ _____
   _____ _____ _____
   _____ _____ _____
   _____ _____ _____
   _____ _____ _____

   c. Sholes purposely created "hurdles" in his design; that is, he placed pairs of letters that are frequently adjacent in requiring the striking by the same hand and even in many cases the same finger (e.g. efficiency, boredom). List ten words that illustrate a "hurdle" on the QWERTY keyboard. List any you discover on the Dvorak keyboard layout.

   QWERTY   Dvorak

   _____ _____   _____ _____
   _____ _____   _____ _____
   _____ _____   _____ _____
   _____ _____   _____ _____
   _____ _____   _____ _____

2. Dvorak received his keyboard patent in 1936 and spent the years of his life working for its acceptance. He died in 1975 without achieving his goal despite documented studies verifying the efficiency of his design. Write a paragraph explaining why you think he was unsuccessful.

_____

_____

_____

_____

_____

_____

_____

_____

3. There has been renewed interest in the Dvorak keyboard with increased use of the electronic keyboard. What steps would you, as an office manager, take to gain acceptance of workers to switching to the new design? Describe a plan for implementation.

_____

_____

_____

_____

_____

_____

_____

_____

4. Can you think of any situations in which the alphabetic layout would be advantageous? Briefly discuss your reasoning.

_____

_____

_____

Software Design

To get the most benefit from the hardware purchased for an information processing system, management must recognize the need to plan for the most efficient use of the software to be used in conjunction with the system. It is of critical importance that every aspect of the human/computer interface be addressed. The design of screen displays, for example, impacts upon the efficiency of both the system and the worker using the system. User-friendly software is more easily integrated with existing systems and is less frustrating for new users to learn. Fewer errors are made when ergonomic guidelines are followed while selecting software and implementing the total system.

PROJECT 1 THAT'S NOT MY JOB—LET THE COMPUTER DO IT!

Objective: to distinguish between those tasks best performed by a computer and those best performed by a human.

Instructions

1. You know that some tasks are performed better by people while other tasks are performed better by a computer. Using the form on page 39, indicate with a check mark whether the task given is best performed by a computer or by a person.

PROJECT 2 PAPER AND SCREEN DISPLAY COMPARISON

Objective: to learn how to analyze and design effective screen and form layouts.

Instructions

1. Compare the paper form and screen display format used in a typical insurance company (see page 38). As you make the comparison, keep in mind that the worker processing the application must look at the information written on the paper form and then key that same information into the computer using the screen format provided.

2. Knowing what you do about formatting, describe any problems that you anticipate the worker keying the information may have. How would you change the form or the screen format to smooth the transition process from printed form to computer input?

PAPER FORM/SCREEN DISPLAY COMPARISON

Handwritten form completed by insurance applicant.

PLEASE PRINT OR TYPE		FOR: ☑ NEW ENROLLMENT ☐ CHANGE COVERAGE			
SOCIAL SECURITY NUMBER 5,3,2 1,4 4,9,6,4	NAME, LAST Peters	FIRST Donald	M.I. W.	☑ MALE ☐ FEMALE	
ADDRESS 1400 Galt Drive	CITY Tamos	STATE Florida	ZIP 33313	☐ SINGLE ☑ MARRIED	
EMPLOYER OR GROUP NAME Info-Tech Industries	TOTAL NUMBER OF DEPENDENTS O	DO YOU WANT DEPENDENT COVERAGE? ☐ YES ☑ NO		☐ RETIRED ☑ ACTIVE	

DO YOU OR ANY OF YOUR DEPENDENTS HAVE OTHER DENTAL COVERAGE? ☐ YES ☑ NO IF YES, COMPLETE SECTION BELOW	HIRE DATE 1-15-88	EFFECTIVE DATE OF COVERAGE 2-1-88
		FOR OFFICE USE ONLY
SOCIAL SECURITY NUMBER	GROUP NUMBER	PROGRAM NUMBER: 57246
NAME OF INSURED		SUBLOCATION NUMBER: 17
EMPLOYER OF INSURED		NUMBER OF DEPENDENTS: O
NAME AND ADDRESS OF OTHER CARRIER		RATE CODE: 02
OTHER INSURANCE COVERS: ☐ INSURED & CHILDREN ☐ INSURED ONLY ☐ INSURED & SPOUSE ☐ INSURED, SPOUSE & CHILDREN		C.O.B. CODES: 14+07

Screen display format.

```
Employer or Group Name ................................................

Hire Date ............................................................

Effective Date of Coverage ........ New Enroll .....................

Program Number ................... Change Coverage ................

S/S No. _ _ _ - _ _ - _ _ _ _    Dependent Group No. ..............

Sublocation ...................... Rate Code ......................

No. of Dependents ................ C.O.B. Codes ...................

M/F  S/M  R/A ...........................

Name, Last ....................... First .......... MI .......

Address .......................... City/State ....... Zip ......

Dependent Coverage  Y   N

Dependent S/S No. _ _ _ - _ _ - _ _ _ _

Name/Address of Other Carrier ........................

Employer of Insured ............... Name of Insured ..............

Other Insurance Covers: Insured & Spouse .... Insured & Children ....

Insured, Spouse, Children ..........................
```

COMPUTER TASKS VERSUS WORKER TASKS

TASK	BEST PERFORMED BY A COMPUTER	BEST PERFORMED BY A PERSON WITHOUT A COMPUTER
1. Proofreading a document for general spelling errors		
2. Searching for accounts that are 90 days overdue		
3. Comparing two screen formats		
4. Predicting future sales based on sales of a product over the past five years		
5. Granting permission for extended payment date		
6. Calculating the effect of a lost account		
7. Proofreading a mailing list of names and addresses		
8. Determining the payback period of an investment		
9. Interpreting breakeven points		
10. Merging several alphabetized lists		
11. Preparing a form letter		
12. Distributing a form letter		
13. Finding a particular source listed in a data base		
14. Changing the abbreviation PSI to Professional Secretaries International in a 12-page report		

The Workstation

Ergonomics plays a vital part in determining what furnishings and layout are appropriate to the task requirements and anthropometric dimensions of the individual workers. By providing appropriate furnishings and accessories, training, and guidelines for rest breaks, managers gain employee support and minimize the possibility of musculoskeletal disorders affecting the office population.

PROJECT 1 TAKE A GOOD LOOK

Objective: to identify elements of workstation design and use.

Instructions

1. Carefully examine the sketch of a typical office worker (page 43).

2. Critique the following aspects of her situation based on the information in Chapter 6 pertaining to posture, musculoskeletal problems, equipment design, and equipment adjustment.

Terminal height   _____

_____

_____

_____

_____

Chair design   _____

_____

_____

_____

Wrist positioning   _____

_____

_____

_____

Work surface layout   _____

_____

_____

_____

_____

PROJECT 2 FIELD RESEARCH — CHAIR EVALUATION

Objective: to help you determine if a chair meets ergonomic guidelines.

Instructions

1. Visit an office furniture store or an office. (Be sure to take with you a tape measure and a protractor.)

2. Use the field research form on page 45. For each of the three chairs you will be evaluating, record the chair model and manufacturer on the top and bottom portions of the form.

3. On the top portion of the field research form, record the measurements for each chair and the specific dimensions for each chair. Then sit in each chair. Record on the bottom of the field research form your ratings and specific comments about each chair.

4. If possible, get a brochure on each of the three chairs before you leave.

5. Complete the evaluation process by comparing the dimensions of each chair that you wrote on the field research form with the ergonomic guidelines given in Chapter 6. Then complete the final evaluation form on page 46. (Refer to the information you recorded on the field research form and the criteria given in Chapter 6.)

PROJECT 3 GIVE YOUR MANAGER SOME HELP

Objective: to learn to adapt a work surface layout to meet a user's needs.

Instructions

1. The placement of equipment and materials within a workstation is determined by the particular job requirements of the user. A job task analysis is a valuable tool for helping to determine what is the proper layout. Review the completed job task analysis on page 47.

2. After you feel you have an understanding of how this manager spends the workday, create a sample layout showing what you feel is the best arrangement to enable the worker to function efficiently within his or her work area. (Cut out the equipment and other items shown on page 49. Glue them onto the work surface shown on page 48.) You should keep in mind that some objects will require less work surface space because they may be stacked (for example, a VDT screen on top of a CPU) or they may stand on end (for example, books on a shelf).

FIELD RESEARCH

CHAIR EVALUATION — PHYSICAL FACTORS RATING

ELEMENT	CHAIR 1 MODEL MANUFACTURER	CHAIR 2 MODEL MANUFACTURER	CHAIR 3 MODEL MANUFACTURER	ERGONOMIC GUIDELINES FROM CHAPTER 6
Seat pan: Height (inches)				16″ to 20.5″
Seat pan: Depth (inches)				15″ to 17″
Seat pan: Width (inches)				18″ to 19″
Seat pan: Tilt (degrees)				0° to 10° forward
Height of lumbar support: (inches)				6″ to 9″ above seat pan
Backrest: Height (inches)				14″ to 16″
Backrest: Width (inches)				10″ to 12″
Backrest: Back/ forth adjustment (inches)				4″ to 6″

CHAIR EVALUATION — SEATING COMFORT RATING

CHAIR 1	CHAIR 2	CHAIR 3
MODEL	MODEL	MODEL
MANUFACTURER	MANUFACTURER	MANUFACTURER
Rating scale (circle one) 1 2 3 4 5	Rating scale (circle one) 1 2 3 4 5	Rating scale (circle one) 1 2 3 4 5
Comments	Comments	Comments

FINAL EVALUATION

1. The best chair was_____for the following reasons:_____

    _____

    _____

    _____

    _____

    _____

    _____

    _____

    _____

    _____

    _____

    _____

2. Comments on the other two chairs: _____

    _____

    _____

    _____

    _____

    _____

    _____

    _____

    _____

    _____

    _____

    _____

WORK SURFACE SELECTION

JOB TASK ANALYSIS QUESTIONNAIRE — WORK SURFACE

Name _Christine Lakovic_

Position/Title _Manager_   Handedness _Left_

1. Please check those items you use.

Monitor	X	Documents:		Labels	
Keyboard	X	8½" x 11"	X	Telephone	X
Disc drive	X	5" x 8"		Calculator	X
Hard disc		3" x 5"		Desk calendar	X
Printer and		Computer listings:		In/Out tray	X
paper feed		11" x 14"	X	Rolodex	X
Graphic tablet		22" x 14"		Document holder	
Mouse		Blueprints		Task light	
Reference manuals	X	File folders	X	Typewriter	

2. Please indicate approximately how many hours each day you spend performing the following tasks.

TASK	1	2	3	4	5+
Using a VDT					
Input from documents					
Input while creating		X			
Input from dictation					
Read/retrieve information on screen					
Input/retrieve from data base while on telephone					
Proof on screen					
Create graphics	X				
Print documents					
Other Tasks at Workstation					
Think/conceptualize		X			
Make/receive phone calls		X			
Write using paper	X				
Proof/review documents	X				
Dictate into a transcriber					
Type using a typewriter					
Use a calculator	X				
Paste-up copy/graphics					
Sort/collate documents/mail					
File	X				
Meet with 1-2 people		X			
Meet with 3 or more people					

WORK SURFACE WORKSHEET

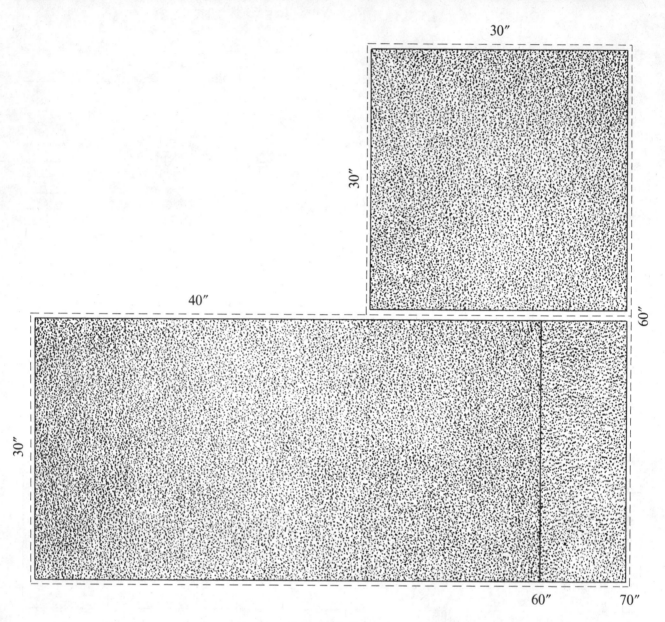

Work Surface

WORK SURFACE EQUIPMENT AND MATERIALS

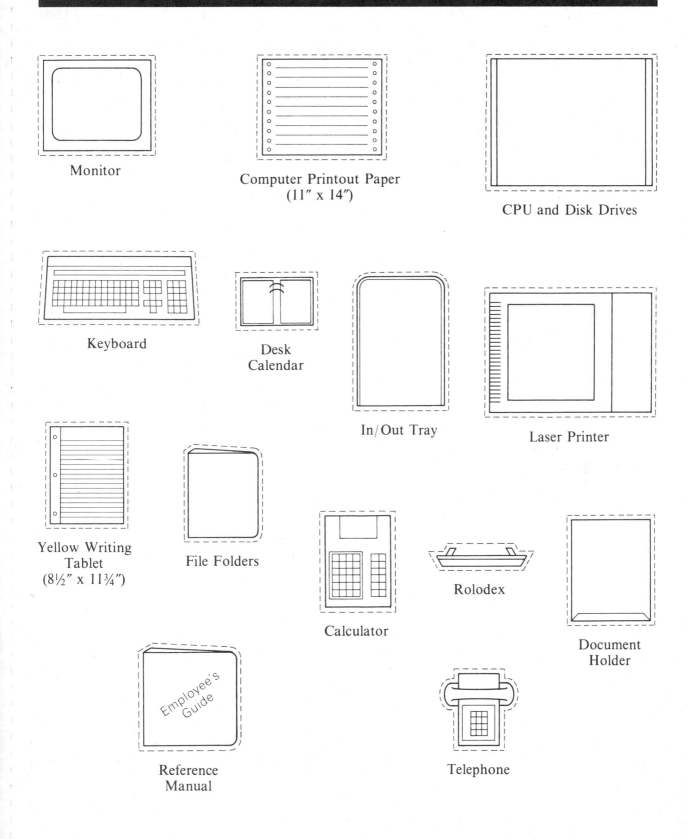

Monitor

Computer Printout Paper
(11″ x 14″)

CPU and Disk Drives

Keyboard

Desk
Calendar

In/Out Tray

Laser Printer

Yellow Writing
Tablet
(8½″ x 11¾″)

File Folders

Calculator

Rolodex

Document
Holder

Reference
Manual

Telephone

The Environment: Space Design

The application of the three major factors of space design (space concept, space layout, and building elements) can greatly contribute to worker performance and job satisfaction. Workers who are encouraged to voice an opinion in regard to how a space is laid out and decorated often feel a sense of ownership and pride in their place of work. An effective project team involves supervisors, management, and staff in the early stages of the design process. Also, it is of critical importance that the space designer understand the uniqueness of the particular office and organization as he/she begins the actual design development.

PROJECT 1 SPACE PLANNING FOR A SMALL FIRM

Objective: to help you apply space planning guidelines to meet the needs of workers.

Instructions

1. Assume that you are charged with planning and making recommendations for the redesign of a space layout for a small accounting firm. Begin by reviewing the job task analysis questionnaire (page 53) completed by Joel Sannoff, Lead Accountant.

2. Then study the notes an ergonomist (page 54) made while visiting on site and conducting interviews with all staff members.

3. Using the grid paper provided on page 55, devise a space plan which takes into account *all* answers to the questions that follow as well as the points raised in the ergonomist's notes.

    Note: The space/privacy requirements, circulation patterns and work flow between individuals indicate the use of a "combination plan." To help you with the process, think through the answers to the following questions:

    • Which workers need to be near each other?

    • Which workers need a closed office space and which workers can be in an open space?

    • Which workers need to be near the photocopy machine?

    • Which workers need easy access to the conference room?

PROJECT 2 FIELD RESEARCH — COLOR PRESENTATION

Objective: to help you apply the information you learned about color.

Instructions

1. Review Chapter 7 of the textbook, especially those sections dealing with color.

2. Visit a travel agency, employment placement service office, insurance company, branch office, or other office that caters to the public. Use the color planning questionnaire on page 57 to collect the relevant data.

3. Plan your color scheme based on the information you gathered from your visit.

4. Collect carpet, fabric, and paint samples from supply stores.

(continued)

5. Mount the samples on a board and indicate where and how the colors are to be used by drawing a simple diagram of the space of the office you visited.

6. Present your color scheme to the class. Justify your selection of colors.

PROJECT 3 SPACE PLANNING FOR A NEW OFFICE

Objective: to help you relate the job function of the workers to the space plan.

Instructions

1. Assume that you are a member of the committee that has been formed to make recommendations about the new office being planned by the pharmaceutical company where you work. You have been asked to concentrate on the research department, in which 28 people work.

   • A department manager is responsible for coordinating the activities of the research department. He meets with them in a conference room.

   • There are ten researchers with Ph.D.'s; their major responsibilities involve working with highly classified information. Two of the researchers coordinate the work of all researchers and are called senior researchers.

   • Each researcher has a computer terminal at his or her workstation; all researchers need easy access to the large company library.

   • There are six research assistants. These workers must share computer terminals in order to access data bases; they also need access to the company library and to the central files.

   • There are two graphic designers who create charts and other visual representations to be included in publications sent to stockholders and to the general public. They also prepare all visual aids used by the researchers when making presentations to various organizations across the country. They need ample storage space for their work.

   • There are five administrative assistants who primarily are responsible for all word processing. One also serves as receptionist. They all do copying and need access to the main printer.

   • The remaining workers are support staff who assist the other workers in a variety of ways, including by using a computer to perform various functions. Some of these workers have computers at their desks; others share a computer.

2. Prepare a report titled "Recommendations for a Space Plan for the Research Department." Assume that management asks you to include the following:

   • a list of people's job functions and the number who perform that function. (i.e. senior researchers, 2; researchers, 8).

   • two bubble diagrams (both intergroup and intragroup) of the research department. Label each bubble with a person's title or function.

   • your recommendations for a closed, open, or combination plan, with the rationale for your suggestions.

   • a simple diagram showing adjacencies with an explanation of your reasons. (Label each workspace with a person's title or function.)

SPACE PLANNING

JOB TASK ANALYSIS QUESTIONNAIRE

Name: ___Joel Sannoff___

Position/Title: ___Lead Accountant___

Please answer the following questions.

1. How many hours a day do you spend in your office? ___5___

2. How many accountants report to you? ___3___

3. How often do you handle confidential information?

   - Daily   ___✓___
   - Once a week   _____
   - Once a month   _____
   - Never   _____

4. What degree of concentration does your work require <u>most</u> of the time?

   - High   ___✓___
   - Some   _____
   - Little   _____

5. How many times a day do you visit other areas?

   - Other workstations ___2___
   - Conference room ___3___
   - Printer/computer room _____
   - Reproduction center _____
   - Reception area ___3___
   - Central file ___2___
   - Library _____
   - Other building _____
   - Secretary's ___3___
     desk

6. a. Which people, by job title, do you interface with most? ___My executive secretary, other accountants, clients___

   b. How often do you meet with them? ___My executive secretary — three times a day, other accountants — usually daily, clients - daily___

SPACE PLANNING

ERGONOMIST'S NOTES

1. Joel indicated the importance of a private corner office with windows for himself.

2. Joel reported that he generally meets with his "special" clients in the conference room.

3. The secretary indicated that 80% *percent* of her work comes from Mr. *Joel* Sannoff.

4. The secretary also serves as receptionist.

5. The three staff accountants work independently with clients at their workstations.

6. They *staff accountants* receive very little secretarial support. They key their own correspondence and use the copy machine as needed.

7. All the accountants start the day with a half-hour meeting in the conference room.

8. Cost containment and careful budgeting were emphasized in the interview.

9. Approximately *twenty* ~~thirty~~ clients visit the office *each* ~~a~~ day.

10. The secretary manages a central file and distributes the files daily according to the scheduling ~~report~~ *calendar*

11. The group does not have any plans for future growth; they like the advantages of being a small operation.

12. ~~The three staff accountants generally eat their lunch in the conference room.~~

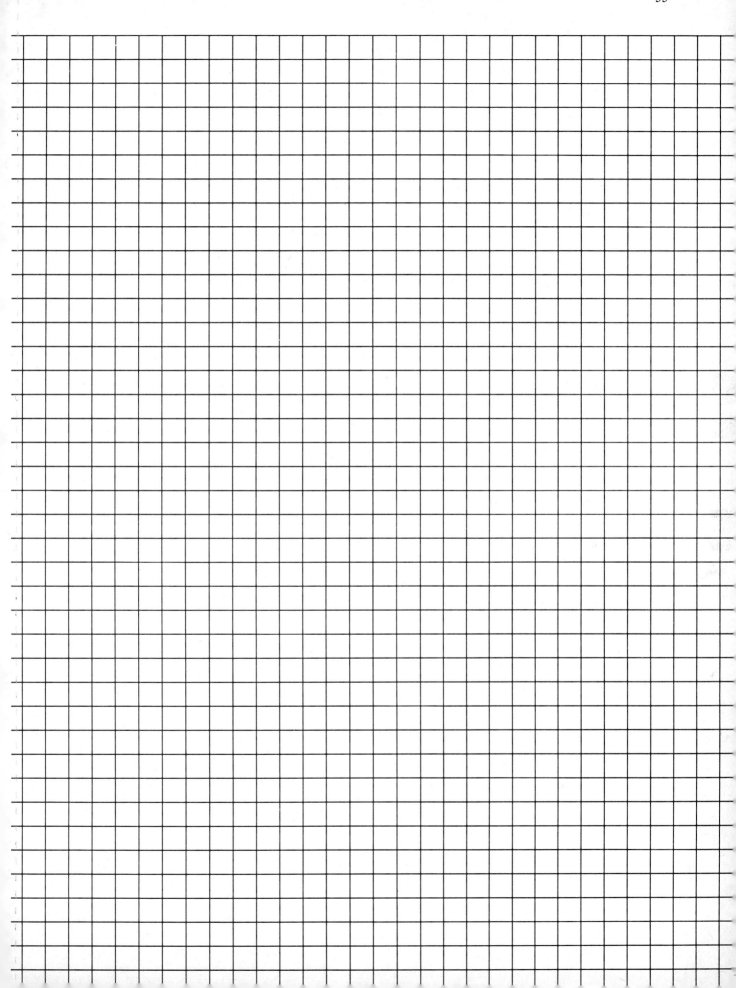

FIELD RESEARCH — COLOR PLANNING

COLOR PLANNING QUESTIONNAIRE

Date of observations _____

Company name _____

Name of contact person_____

1. How many walls have windows? _____

    What direction (north, south, east, west) do the windows (if any) face?_____

2. How would you describe the apparent *mood* in this office? _____

    _____

    Explain your answer _____

    _____

    _____

3. What type of overhead lighting exists? _____

    _____

    _____

    _____

4. Is task lighting used?_____

    _____

    _____

    _____

    _____

5. Do all employees talk with clients?_____

    If no, list some of the other activities you observed. _____

    _____

    _____

    _____

    _____

(continued)

6. How extensively are computers used? _____

_____

_____

7. Approximately how large is the area in which clients/customers talk with employees? _____

_____

8. Are meetings held in closed offices? In a large open area in which there are several desks? __

_____

_____

_____

9. What are the dimensions of (a) the entire work area? _____ (b) the typical individual office? _____ (c) the typical individual workstation? _____ and (d) the reception area? _____

10. How far must a client/customer walk from the reception area to the office or workstation of the company employee with whom he or she deals? _____

_____

_____

_____

11. What traffic patterns are evident? _____

_____

_____

12. What colors are in use now? _____

_____

_____

13. What colors does the manager like? _____

_____

_____

The Environment: Lighting, Acoustics, Thermal Comfort, and Air Quality

Office automation has greatly complicated environmental considerations in planning office space. Management must look seriously into all the issues affecting the workplace environment. Problems can be avoided when lighting and acoustical needs are examined carefully. The controlling of light and noise sources can provide optimal work conditions. In addition, terminal comfort and air quality can be affected by advanced technology and, if ignored, will ultimately affect worker performance.

PROJECT 1 ENVIRONMENTAL INTERVIEW

Objective: to help you become aware of the environmental issues in an office.

Instructions

1. Arrange to interview a company safety officer, industrial hygienist, or plant and facilities manager to discuss lighting, noise, and thermal comfort of a designated office. (Ask if you may tour the office as you conduct the interview.)

2. Conduct the interview, using the questionnaire provided on page 61. Do not feel that you are limited to asking only those questions on the questionnaire. Ask any additional questions you may have with regard to lighting, noise, and thermal comfort.

3. Your instructor may ask you to share your findings as part of a general class discussion.

PROJECT 2 THE MIRROR TEST

Objective: to identify sources of glare, which is the best means of preventing visual discomfort.

Instructions

1. Using a hand mirror, conduct the following mirror test on five different VDT screens; complete the glare analysis form on page 63 as you conduct each test.

    • Sit in front of the terminal screen (any display may be on the screen).

    • Locate *on the screen* any evidences of glare.

    • Place a hand mirror directly on top of the glare spot.

    • Reflected in the mirror you will see the source of the glare (overhead light, task light, window, etc.).

2. Using the glare analysis form on page 63, make specific recommendations for eliminating the glare. (If necessary, refer to Chapter 8.)

PROJECT 3 TIGHT BUILDING SYNDROME

Objective: to recognize the environmental problems in some new buildings.

Instructions

Read the article on pages 65-69 titled "Tight Building Syndrome: When Work Makes You Sick." Then answer the following questions.

1. Based on the information in the article regarding the symptoms of tight building syndrome, what steps would you take as an office manager to distinguish between common ailments such as hay fever and colds and those which may be symptoms of the syndrome?

    _____

    _____

    _____

    _____

2. What potential sources of air contaminants should you consider in guiding an investigation in an office when tight building syndrome is suspected?

    _____

    _____

    _____

    _____

    _____

    _____

3. What does ASHRAE stand for? _____

4. If, as an office manager, you were to use a questionnaire such as the one included in the article, how would you prepare the employees before distributing it?

    _____

    _____

    _____

5. If the collation of the questionnaires indicated a high percentage of complaints, what steps would you take to improve the situation?

    _____

    _____

    _____

ENVIRONMENTAL INTERVIEW

ENVIRONMENTAL ISSUES QUESTIONNAIRE

Title of person interviewed _____

Company name _____

LIGHTING

1. What are possible sources of glare within the computer users' fields of vision? _____

    _____

    _____

2. Are the operators' fields of vision free of reflections from the screen, keyboard, papers, etc.?

    _____

3. Are there internal and/or external blinds on windows? _____

4. Is the general level of lighting adjustable?_____

5. Is there a need for task lighting? _____

6. Are lamps or fixtures designed so lamps will not flicker prior to burning out?_____

    _____

7. Are lamps and fixtures regularly cleaned and maintained? _____

8. Do diffusers adequately control glare? _____

Other comments _____

_____

_____

_____

NOISE

1. What are the possible sources of noise within the computer users' hearing ranges?_____

2. Have high frequency tones been eliminated from the noise environment? _____

3. Are there external sources of noise? Can these be controlled (if technical measurements are available)?

    _____

4. Is the noise level less than 55 db(A)* in work areas requiring high concentration, and less than 65 db(A) elsewhere? _____

5. Are equipment noise levels no greater than 5 db(A) than the surrounding noise level? _____

*db = decibel, a measure of sound intensity. Human speech is appoximately 80 decibels.

(continued)

Other comments _____

_____

_____

_____

THERMAL COMFORT

1. Can room temperature be adjusted or maintained at a constant level? _____

2. Is the room air-conditioned? _____

3. Can humidity be controlled or maintained at a constant level? _____

4. Have "hot spots" been eliminated?

Other comments _____

_____

_____

_____

GLARE ANALYSES FORM

TERMINAL 1

Location of Terminal _____

Source of Glare _____

_____

Recommendation _____

_____

_____

_____

_____

TERMINAL 2

Location of Terminal _____

Source of Glare _____

_____

Recommendation _____

_____

_____

_____

_____

TERMINAL 3

Location of Terminal _____

Source of Glare _____

_____

Recommendation _____

_____

_____

_____

_____

(continued)

TERMINAL 4

Location of Terminal _____

Source of Glare _____

_____

Recommendation _____

_____

_____

_____

_____

_____

_____

_____

TERMINAL 5

Location of Terminal _____

Source of Glare _____

_____

Recommendation _____

_____

_____

_____

_____

_____

_____

_____

Tight Building Syndrome: When Work Makes You Sick

Energy-efficient designs for office buildings leave workers tired, congested . . . and complaining

Indoor, non-industrial environments such as modern office buildings and homes commonly are considered to be free of overt health hazards. In recent years, however, health complaints have arisen in certain new office buildings and the phrase "Tight Building Syndrome" is becoming more common.

Most of these buildings are tight, energy-efficient designs with outside air provided through recirculating air-conditioning systems. As advantageous as the design seemed to be originally, hidden problems have been surfacing.

Tight building syndrome is characterized by a significant number of building occupants complaining of specific health complaints common in these building investigations. As of yet, there have only been a few published studies on the syndrome.[1,2]

Table 1 lists some symptoms and complaints noted in several investigations. The most common complaints include eye, nose and throat irritation, headache, fatigue, sneezing and difficulty in wearing contact lenses.

Most individuals say the severity of their discomfort increases as the day progresses, and many state a similar trend over the course of a week. Most notice a dramatic improvement in their condition after being out of the building for a short period of time—sometimes for as short as 15 minutes.

Attack rates for particular episodes vary considerably—approaching 70 percent of the total

By Jeff B. Hicks, CIH, *Industrial Hygienist, Fireman's Fund Insurance Companies, Sacramento, Calif.*

population of one building—as determined by using health questionnaires filled out by the occupants. In other investigations, only certain individuals located in specific building areas have experienced common symptoms.

As these symptoms resemble common ailments, including hay fever and colds, building administrators and managers often fail to respond until employees have complained repeatedly, sometimes to the point of exasperation and anger. In these situations, it is often difficult to obtain an objective evaluation of the number and type of symptoms as emotional reaction to the specific symptoms comes into play. These reactions, however, may be additional symptoms of the syndrome.[3]

The explanation of hayfever or the common cold as the source of problems in these buildings is not a sufficient explanation. The symptoms are quite common from one building to another and often disappear within minutes of the individual leaving the building. Additionally, the symptoms persist when ambient pollen counts are low and individuals are asymptomatic when away from the building.

AIR CONTAMINANTS. The most common inference made by health investigators and building occupants experiencing discomfort is that some air contaminants are present and cause the problem. Initial investigations into these buildings were based on a collection of air samples in an attempt to identify the specific causal agents.

Using traditional industrial hygiene sampling and analytical techniques, only a few con-

taminants, in extremely low concentrations, were identified. By increasing sensitivity of specific methods, more compounds were identified, although concentrations were so low it was impossible to correlate these with the observed effects.

Table 2 lists concentrations of detected air contaminants from one tight building syndrome investigation. Airborne concentrations were uniformly higher inside the buildings than in comparison samples collected outside.

Extensive air sampling programs in a number of tight building syndrome investigations have yet to detect air contaminants at concentrations exceeding, or even approaching, any Threshold Limit Value, OSHA Permissible Exposure Limit or NIOSH Recommended Standard.

For the majority of the contaminants detected, the measured concentrations were 100 to 1,000 times lower than the appropriate airborne standard.

Some interesting results were obtained concerning the presence of organic vapors using a highly sensitive technique. Office air, as well as outside control air, was passed through purged Tenax® or Poropac® (solid sorbents) followed by thermal desorption into a liquid nitrogen trap and subsequent analysis of the collected condensate by high resolution gas chromatograph/mass spectrometer.

By this method, more than 30 different organic species inside problem buildings have been identified, as compared to outdoor samples.

Table 3 lists organics detected by this technique. Again, the concentrations are so low as to defy interpretation, but the number of different organic species detected by this method suggest some association. Others have discovered similar substances in office environments.[4,5]

Airborne carbon dioxide (CO_2) gas generated by human respiration and tobacco smoke and carbon monoxide (CO) gas from tobacco smoke are useful indicators of the adequacy of outside fresh dilution air ventilation.[6]

In measuring CO_2 and CO concentrations continuously in problem buildings, we have observed carbon dioxide concentrations treble over the course of the day, with carbon monoxide concentrations doubling.

Table 4 illustrates that the concentrations of these "indicator gases" are higher in the afternoon than in the morning. The severity of symptoms in complaining individuals generally is worse in the afternoon than in the morning, suggesting a correlation with the observed increased concentration of these indictor gases, and likely other contaminants as well.

SOURCES. The sources of air contaminants detected in our investigations are not always obvious. Tobacco smoke is the most apparent source for a variety of substances, most notably carbon monoxide, oxides of nitrogen, aldehydes (e.g. formaldehyde), polynuclear aromatic hydrocarbons, and airborne particulates.[7]

The presence of low-level solvent vapors is more difficult to explain. Large varieties of adhesives commonly are employed in modern building construction (e.g. tile, carpet and floor adhesives) and many contain solvents. Adhesives also are used in the manufacture of office furniture and fixtures. Office equipment, such as copy machines and computer printers, janitorial supplies, such as insecticides and fungicides, and other activities common to office buildings all add

to the presence of air contaminants. The individual or combined impact of these contaminants on the health of occupants is not known.

Heating, ventilation and air conditioning (HVAC) in most modern office buildings is provided by an air-recirculating system designed to provide outside "clean" air, yet recirculating large quantities of pre-conditioned air, to conserve energy.

Some systems employ the use of heat-exchangers that transfer the thermal load from one body of warm (or cool) air to fresh, incoming air. Windows typically are caulked and cannot be opened. This is done to restrict outside air infiltration and to maintain energy-efficient operation that may be compromised by opened windows.

It is estimated that of the total energy consumed by our nation, approximately 10 percent is used for

---

Many workers report discomfort increases as the day progresses.

---

heating and cooling air in homes and offices.[8] The need to utilize energy-efficient ventilation systems is obvious.

In many building ventilation systems, the quantity of outside make-up air is dictated by an automatic damper system; temperature and humidity-probes inside and outside the building prescribe the quantity of outside air that enters the building according to building needs and ambient conditions for most efficient operation. These systems usually provide a minimum quantity of fresh, outside air, even at the most restricted damper setting.

STANDARDS. Ventilation system design and operational standards, as well as minimum fresh outside air (OA) requirements, are provided by the American Society of Heating, Refrigerating & Air Conditioning Engineers (ASHRAE). Many buildings constructed during

the last six years were based on ventilation design criteria set forth in ASHRAE 62-73, "Indoor Ventilation Standards," published in 1977.[9]

This standard recommended that a minimum of 2.5 liters per second (1/s) OA be provided per person (or 5 cubic feet per minute, per person) for a typical open office setting with adequate air filtration and temperature controls.

More recently, ASHRAE has published 62-1981, "Ventilation For Acceptable Indoor Air Quality," updating and modifying the previous standard for building ventilation and indoor air quality.[10]

The new ASHRAE standard provides an alternative method to minimum OA ventilation rates based on determining and maintaining contaminant concentrations within established limits. It also requires higher OA ventilation where tobacco smoking is permitted. In a typical office building where smoking is permitted, a minimum of 10 1/s (20 CFM) OA per person now is recommended—a fourfold increase in fresh air requirements over the 62-73 standard.

Investigations have indicated tight building syndrome occurs more frequently in buildings where ventilation rates are maintained near the minimum 2.5 1/s OA per person. However, similar symptoms and complaints were observed in buildings where ventilation rates were approximately three times higher (7 1/s OA per person).

In several investigations, operational characterisitcs of the ventilation system resulted in lowered OA ventilation rates below the ASHRAE minimum. The use of indicator gas measurements to assess adequacy of outside dilution fresh air and to determine the quantity of air entering the HVAC system are an essential aspect of investigating suspect tight buildings.

Air quality improvements, measured in terms of fewer individuals reporting symptoms, have been observed when OA ventilation rates have been upgraded to meet ASHRAE 62-1981 recommendations for offices permitting tobacco smoking, 10 1/s OA per person. Ventilation plays an important role in tight building syndrome.

Table 5 reviews some OA ventilation rates measured before and after changes in the systems operation, and resultant attack rates of the syndrome's symptoms.

Unfortunately, not all studied buildings have experienced significant relief following increased OA ventilation rates, even when conforming to ASHRAE 62-1981 standards.

Investigation of any reported health hazard associated with air contamination, with few clues implicating specific agents, is a difficult and often frustrating endeavor. Over the course of several investigations, a protocol has been developed to streamline investigations of tight building syndrome to help eliminate unnecessary procedures.

SYMPTOMS. An essential starting point to any building-related outbreak of illness is to completely

Office Health Questionnaire

Some individuals working in this office building have registered health complaints. To help investigate the possible presence, or absence, of these complaints, this questionnaire is being distributed to all occupants. Your assistance is requested. Please complete this questionnaire as accurately as possible. Return in a sealed envelope to the building manager. Thank you for your assistance.

1. **COMPLAINTS:** (select choices that may be related to your presence in this building. This is a random list—not all complaints listed have been noted in this building).

    ____Aching joints
    ____Muscle twitching
    ____Back pain
    ____Hearing disturbances
    ____Dizziness
    ____Dry, flaking skin
    ____Discolored skin
    ____Skin irritation/itching
    ____Heartburn
    ____Nausea
    ____Noticeable odors
    ____Sinus congestion
    ____Sneezing
    ____Chest tightness
    ____Eye irritation
    ____Problems wearing contact lenses
    ____Headache
    ____Fatigue/drowsiness
    ____Temperature too hot
    ____Temperature too cold
    ____Other (specify)_____

2. **WHEN DO THESE COMPLAINTS OCCUR?**
    ____Morning
    ____Afternoon
    ____All day
    ____Daily
    ____Specific day(s) of the week
    ____No noticeable trend

3. **WHEN DO YOU EXPERIENCE RELIEF FROM THESE COMPLAINTS?**

    _____

    _____

4. **DO YOU HAVE ANY OF THE FOLLOWING?**
    (Please check positive responses)
    ____Hay fever, pollen allergies
    ____Skin allergies/dermatitis
    ____Other allergies
    ____Cold/flu
    ____Sinus problems

5. **DO YOU SMOKE TOBACCO?**
    ____Yes
    ____No
    ____Amount

6. **ON WHAT FLOOR OF THE BUILDING ARE YOU LOCATED?** _____
    WHAT DEPARTMENT OR AREA?_____
    ARE YOU NEAR ANY OFFICE EQUIPMENT?

    (specify) _____

7. **COMMENTS OR OBSERVATIONS:**

    _____

    _____

NAME (optional):

    _____

characterize the symptoms and complaints, their distribution in terms of the person, their location and relative time. A health questionnaire completed by all individuals within the problem building is the most practical and simplest method to acquire this information. Figure 1 is an example of such a questionnaire.

This questionnaire elicits specific symptoms and other complaints: where the employee is located, when the symptoms developed and when relief is experienced and possible confounding factors. The questionnaire must be short and simple to complete and score for acceptability by both employees and management.

Relative attack rates for specific symptoms may be calculated and areas where symptoms are notably worse or better are detected. Unusual complaints or symptoms may be identified to assist in the investigation.

Monitoring symptom attack-rates by using health questionnaires following modifications that may affect the airborne environment,

---

A questionnaire for all employees best way to find problem.

---

such as increasing building OA ventilation, may help demonstrate its effectiveness, or lack thereof.

Increasing the amount of outside air that enters the building is a common recommendation, which substantially increases energy usage and costs. The documentation of its success may convince management to accept increased operating costs.

Often building managers are reluctant to utilize the questionnaires, as they believe it may alert non-affected employees, assuring liability or stimulating workmen's compensation claims. In buildings where questionnaires have been used, this has not happened.

Typically, the number of complaining employees is quite high, and most employees already are

aware of the presence of health complaints in the building. The questionnaires demonstrate that management is concerned and is seeking solutions.

Good communications with all individuals in the building by discussing the suspected problems, and actions being taken, will help alleviate concern.

If management adamantly rejects the use of health questionnaires, absentee rates may give some indication of the extent and severity of the problem. This information also is useful when building management fails to realize a problem exists. This method may be useful only where the office environment has been altered recently, such as with new carpet, furniture or a move to a new office or building.

Health questionnaires should be administered on a regular basis. Initially, emotional responses may complicate the interpretation of the questionnaires. Having them filled out on a regular basis will help temper such responses and provide a baseline from which effects of future modifications can be assessed more accurately.

VENTILATION. If the health questionnaire or interviews with complaining individuals suggests a pattern consistent with tight building syndrome, a detailed evaluation of the ventilation system is warranted. This examination should consider operation of the system at design specifications, determine the quantity of outside air provided per person under varying temperature demand conditions and examine any in-line air-cleaning equipment.

Measuring indicator gases, CO and CO_2, also is considered part of the ventilation evaluation as it will assess if sufficient quantities of dilution air are being provided to the building and preventing these gases from accumulating throughout the day.

Direct-reading carbon monoxide monitors with a strip-chart recorder for continuous monitoring are commonly applied in studies. Direct

Table 1

Common Tight Building Syndrome Symptoms

Eye irritation	Chest tightness
Sinus congestion	Sneezing
Headache	Nausea
Fatigue	Dizziness
Difficulty with	Dermatitis
wearing contact lenses	

Table 2

Air Contaminants Detected in Tight Building Investigations

Substance	Concentration (ug/m³)
Total dust	20-40
Respirable dust	10-25
Coal Tar Pitch Volatiles	0.05-0.2
	(ppb)
Formaldehyde	5-40
Toluene	10-30
o,m,p-Xylene	10-20
Ethylbenzene	5-15
Hexane	10-25
1,1,1,-Trichloroethane	50-150
1,1,2,2-Perchloroethylene	40-80
C_7-C_{11} Alkanes	10-50
Ozone	5-10
NOx	200
Carbon Monoxide	2-5 ppm
Carbon Dioxide	0.05-0.09%

reading indicator tubes that take samples every half-hour to assess any accumulation of carbon dioxide also are used.

If deficiencies in the building ventilation design or operation are noted with respect to the ASHRAE 62-1981 standard, the system should be upgraded to meet the standards. Measure the effect of the changes by a follow-up health questionnaire, and if possible, do not inform the occupants of any changes to enhance the objectivity of the questionnaire.

Initial studies of health complaints in office buildings consisted of utilizing the industrial hygienist's most powerful technique in investigating health hazards—air sampling and analysis for suspected air contaminants. Yet, after collection and analysis of hundreds of indoor air samples, in most cases by sensitive and expensive techniques, specific agents in concentrations that would explain the observed symptoms have not been identified.

If health questionnaires have documented a high number of complaints in an office building, and the ventilation evaluation indicates adequate quantities of outside air ventilation, only then should air sampling and analysis be conducted for unidentified contaminants.

Formaldehyde is the most common contaminant sampled for in these buildings. Most modern office buildings do not use many materials containing formaldehyde products, however, so the usefulness of this investigation technique is questionable.

Several reports have identified sodium dodecyl sulfate, a component of many carpet shampoos, as the causal agent associated with upper respiratory tract and eye irritation in certain offices.[11,12] Airborne solvent vapors off-gasing from an adhesive, used to install a new carpet, produced similar symptoms.[13]

Where specific or unusual symptoms are noted and potential sources have been identified as possible contaminants, air sampling and analysis definitely are warranted.

RESEARCH NEEDS. The etiology of tight building syndrome is not understood. A wide variety of low-level air contaminants have been detected in these buildings, but their significance is not clear. Well-organized and supported research involving epidemiology, industrial hygiene and ventilation engineering disciplines must be involved before an understanding of the specific conditions associated with causes and methods to eliminate these health complaints can be gained.

ASHRAE has issued a position statement concerning indoor air quality and recommended that research efforts be increased substantially to promote an understanding of the indoor en-

vironments where most of us spend the majority of our time.[14]

The American Conference of Governmental Industrial Hygienists is forming an Indoor Office En-

vironment Committee to review the current understanding of these office building complaints and, hopefully, to shed some light on causes and solutions.

Table 3

Organics Detected by GC/MS in Tight Building Syndrome Investigations

1,1,1-Tricholoroethane	n-Hexadecane	2-Hexanone
1,1,2,2-Perchlorethylene	5-Penyldecane	3-Heptanone
Cyclohexane	Toluene	Butylcyclohexane
n-Heptane	Ethylbenzene	Naphthalene
n-Octane	o,m,p-Xylene	n-Butylacetate
n-Nonane	Propylbenzene	Limonene
n-Decane	1-Ethyl-2-methylbenzene	Carvone
n-Dodecane	1-Ethyl-4-methylbenzene	1-Methylnaphthalene
n-Tridecane	C^3-Alkyl benzenes	Ethylsilane
n-Pentadecane	Cyclohexanol	Menthone

Table 4

CO and CO_2 Concentrations Variations with Time

Time of Day	CO(ppm)	CO_2 (% by volume)
0700	2.0	0.030
0800	2.0	0.035
0900	2.3	0.055
1000	2.5	0.060
1100	3.1	0.070
1200	2.5	0.075
1300	3.1	0.080
1400	3.5	+0.090
1500	4.1	0.070
1600	4.0	0.065
1700	+4.2	0.060
1800	3.1	0.050
1900	2.4	0.050
2000	2.1	0.040
2100	2.0	0.050

+peak concentrations

References

1. Kreiss, K.: Building-Associated Epidemics, in Indoor Air Quality (P.J. Walsh and C.S. Dudney, eds.) CRC Press, Boca Raton, Florida, (1983).
2. Turiel, I., M.J. Coye, et al: The Effects of Reduced Ventilation on Indoor Air Quality in an Office Building, Lawrence Berkeley Laboratories, *LBL Report* 10379, Berkeley (1981).
3. Faust, H.S. and M.B. Brilliant: Is the diagnosis of "Mass Hysteria" an Excuse for Incomplete Investigation of Low-Level Environmental Contamination. *J. Occupational Medicine* 23:22-26 (1981).
4. Schmidt, H.E., C.D. Hollowell, et al: Trace Organics in Offices. Lawrence Berkeley Laboratories, *LBL Report* 11378, Berkeley (1980).
5. Johansson, I.: Determination of Organic Compounds in Indoor Air with Potential Reference to Air Quality. *Atmospheric Environment* 12:1371-1377 (1978).
6. Turiel, I., and J. Rudy: Occupant-Generated CO_2 as an Indicator of Ventilation Rate, Lawrence Berkeley Laboratories, *LBL Report* 10496, Berkeley (1980).
7. National Research Council: Indoor Pollutants, pp. 149-168, National Academy Press, Washington (1981).
8. Jackson, J.R. and W.S. Johnson: Commercial Energy Use: A Disaggregation by Fuel, Building Type, and End Use. Oak Ridge National Laboratory, *ORNL/CON-14,* Tennessee (1978).
9. American Society of Heating, Refrigerating and Air Conditioning Engineers (ASHRAE): Standards for Natural and Mechanical Ventilation (ASHRAE 62-73), Atlanta (1977).
10. ASHRAE: Ventilation for Acceptable Indoor Air Quality (ASHRAE Standard 62-1981), Atlanta (1981).
11. Kreiss, K., M.G. Gonzales, et al: Respiratory Irritation Due to Carpet Shampoo. Chronic Diseases Division, Center for Environmental Health, Centers for Disease Control, Atlanta (1981).
12. Persoff, R. and M. Koketsu: Respiratory Irritation and Carpet Shampoo, in Proc. Fifth Inter. Symp. Medichem, (C. Hine and D.J. Killian, eds.) p. 347, San Francisco (1977).
13. University of Washington, School of Public Health and Community Medicine: Indoor Air Problems—The Office Environment, in *Environmental Health and Safety News* (P.A. Breysee, ed.) 30:1-17, Seattle (1982).
14. ASHRAE: *Position Statement of Indoor Air Quality,* Atlanta (1982).

Source: Hicks, Jeff B. "Tight Building Syndrome: When Work Makes You Sick," *Occupational Health and Safety*, January 1984: 51–55.

Chapter 9   Projects

Training

Training within an organization can set the tone for ergonomic implementation and really get things "rolling." It is essential in settings where technology is being introduced as well as in those environments with existing systems. Training is important for executives, managers, supervisors, and the VDT users themselves. Training for the automated office should include system and skills training, information on environmental and psychosocial issues, and strategies for effectively dealing with stress, fatigue, and visual and musculoskeletal problems associated with computer work. Using the principles of andragogy and the established process for training development ensures that training will be appropriately presented and designed to meet the particular needs of an organization.

PROJECT 1 HOW DOES YOUR CLASS RATE?

Objective: to determine the effectiveness of a class from a training perspective.

Instructions

1. It has been said that training is the process by which people acquire the knowledge, skills, and mental attitudes that enable them to perform their jobs. Some of the courses you are now taking (courses that are directly related to your career goals) can be considered a form of training. Select a career-related course in which you are currently enrolled and evaluate its effectiveness from a training perspective.

2. Complete the course rating sheet on page 73. Use a circle to indicate your rating of each factor, with a rating of 5 being the highest or best rating and 1 being the lowest. Note that space is provided for you to write comments and/or examples to justify your rating.

PROJECT 2 EVALUATING TRAINING SITUATIONS

Objective: to evaluate the applications of adult learning theory in sample situations.

Instructions

1. Read "Characteristics and Implications of Adult Learning Theory" presented in chart form by Malcolm Knowles (page 72).

2. Read the four training situations described on pages 75 and 76. For each scenario, determine whether the implications presented in the Knowles chart have been violated or reinforced. (Use a check mark to indicate your evaluation.) Then state in your own words at least one of the "implications for adult learning" that was either violated or reinforced.

3. Finally, identify at least one of the "implications for presentors" that should guide the trainer in handling the particular situation described in the scenario; be sure to explain the relevance of the implication.

PROJECT 3 DEVELOPING A SHORT TRAINING SEMINAR

Objective: to apply principles for developing training to a short seminar on ergonomics.

Instructions

You are director of corporate training for a major airline. You are given responsibility for planning and conducting a two-day ergonomics seminar for 15 customer service supervisors. Twenty customer service reservationists report to each supervisor. Customer service reservationists are full-time computer users; the supervisors are part-time computer users. Complete the five steps given (pages 77–79) for planning your seminar.

CHARACTERISTICS AND IMPLICATIONS OF ADULT LEARNING THEORY

Characteristics of Adult Learners	Implications for Adult Learning	Implications for Presentors
Self Concept: The adult learner sees himself as capable of self-direction and desires others to see him the same way. In fact, one definition of maturity is the capacity to be self-directing.	• A climate of openness and respect is helpful in identifying what the learners want and need to learn. • Adults enjoy planning and carrying out their own learning exercises. • Adults need to be involved in evaluating their own progress toward self-chosen goals.	Presentors recognize participants as self-directing . . . and treat them accordingly. The presentor is a learning reference for the participants rather than a traditional instructor; presentors are, therefore, encouraged to "tell it like it is" and stress "how I do it" rather than tell participants what they should do. The presentor avoids "talking down" to participants who are experienced decision-makers and self-starters. The presentor instead tries to meet the participants' needs.
Experience: Adults bring a lifetime of experience to the learning situation. Youths tend to regard experience as something that has happened to them, while to an adult, his experience is him. The adult defines who he is in terms of his experience.	• Less use is made of transmittal techniques; more of experiential techniques. • Discovery of how to learn from experience is key to self-actualization. • Mistakes are opportunities for learning. • To reject adult experience is to reject the adult.	As the adult is his experience, failure to utilize the experience of the adult learner is equivalent to rejecting him as a person.
Readiness-to-Learn: Adult developmental tasks increasingly move toward social and occupational role competence and away from the more physical developmental tasks of childhood.	• Adults need opportunities to identify the competency requirements of their occupational and social roles. • Adult readiness-to-learn and teachable moments peak at those points where a learning opportunity is coordinated with a recognition of the need-to-know. • Adults can best identify their own readiness-to-learn and teachable moments.	Learning occurs through helping participants with the identification of gaps in the learner's knowledge. No questions are "stupid"; all questions are "opportunities" for learning.
A problem-centered time perspective: Youth thinks of education as the accumulation of knowledge for use in the future. Adults tend to think of learning as a way to be more effective in problem solving today.	• Adult education needs to be problem-centered rather than theoretically oriented. • Formal curriculum development is less valuable than finding out what the learners need to learn. • Adults need the opportunity to apply and try out learning quickly.	The primary emphasis in the course is on students learning rather than on teachers teaching. Involvement in such things as problems to be solved, case histories, and critical incidents generally offer greater learning opportunity for adults than "talking to" them.

COURSE RATING SHEET

COURSE NAME _____

	RATING (circle one)	COMMENT/EXAMPLES
TRAINING PRINCIPLES		
• Stimulates your "need to know"	1 2 3 4 5	
• Encourages you to be responsible for your learning	1 2 3 4 5	
• Relates to your experiences	1 2 3 4 5	
• Uses a problem-solving approach to real life situations	1 2 3 4 5	
• Provides for individual differences in learning styles, pace, and training	1 2 3 4 5	
FACILITATOR'S ROLE		
• Provides practice of ideas presented	1 2 3 4 5	
• Appeals to your senses using lecture, visual materials, kinesthetic stimuli	1 2 3 4 5	
• Rewards correct responses immediately with praise	1 2 3 4 5	
• Keeps you active (activities, discussions)	1 2 3 4 5	

ADULT TRAINING SITUATIONS

SITUATION 1

A trainer who represents a newly installed software program called "Copyend" is meeting with the supervisors who will be training their subordinates to use the program. The trainer begins the session by asking the supervisors what kind of training (if any) they have conducted in the past.

Implications for adult learning
_____ have been violated.

Implications for adult learning
_____ have been reinforced.

Implication for adult learning:_____

_____

_____

_____

Implication for presenter: _____

_____

_____

_____

SITUATION 2

A training class is being conducted on "Active Listening Skills." A participant asks the trainer a question on techniques that had just been covered in detail five minutes ago. The trainer laughs out loud and says, "My, you obviously need this class, don't you?" and immediately moved on to the next point on the course outline.

Implications for adult learning
_____ have been violated.

Implications for adult learning
_____ have been reinforced.

Implication for adult learning:_____

_____

_____

_____

Implication for presenter: _____

_____

_____

_____

(continued)

SITUATION 3

A well-known speaker in the field of industrial hygiene is about to make a highly technical presentation to all the customer service representatives of a large utilities company. The title of the presentation is "Hazards of Today's Workplace." Before beginning to speak, the industrial hygienist distributes to the customer service representatives a glossary of technical terms with definitions any layperson could understand. Then she says, "Those of us in the field of industrial hygiene tend to use some long, complicated-sounding words. But once you get past the spelling of the terms, you'll find the meanings are pretty simple."

Implications for adult learning
_____ have been violated.

Implications for adult learning
_____ have been reinforced.

Implication for adult learning:_____

_____

_____

_____

Implication for presentor:_____

_____

_____

_____

SITUATION 4

A successful retired businessperson is addressing a group of small business owners at a local chamber of commerce luncheon meeting. His topic is "How to Run A Business the Easy Way." The businessperson uses many personal anecdotes as he shares with his audience his formula for success in business.

Implications for adult learning
_____ have been violated.

Implications for adult learning
_____ have been reinforced.

Implication for adult learning:_____

_____

_____

_____

Implication for presentor:_____

_____

_____

_____

SEMINAR PLANNING PROCEDURES

STEP 1

Read again that portion of Chapter 9 that deals with "Procedures for Developing Training" and "The Trainer as Facilitator." Also review any additional chapters in the text that contain information about ergonomics you may wish to include in your seminar.

STEP 2

There must be clear goals and objectives for the seminar you are developing. List below your primary goal and two objectives for the seminar.

GOAL _____

_____

_____

Objective _____

_____

_____

_____

Objective _____

_____

_____

_____

_____

STEP 3

You must have a general idea of the content to be covered in the seminar. List here the major topics you feel must be covered. (Do not worry yet about the order in which they will be covered.)

Topics to be covered

_____   _____

_____   _____

_____   _____

_____   _____

_____   _____

(continued)

STEP 4

Once you have listed the basic topics you wish to cover, you must then develop the course. Complete the form provided on page 79 to finalize the outline and identify the instructional methodology and audiovisual materials you will use to conduct the seminar. (NOTE: Instructional methodology, for example, might be lecture, group discussion, working in pairs, and demonstration. Audiovisual materials, for example, might be slides, transparencies, magazine articles, handouts, flip-charts, and equipment manuals. You may add or subtract numerals and letters in order to accommodate your final outline.)

STEP 5

Briefly discuss how you plan to evaluate whether or not the training was successful in meeting the goals you listed in Step 2 of these seminar planning procedures.

_____

_____

_____

_____

_____

_____

_____

_____

_____

_____

_____

_____

_____

_____

_____

_____

ERGONOMICS SEMINAR FOR AIRLINE CUSTOMER SERVICE SUPERVISORS

OUTLINE	METHODOLOGY	AUDIOVISUAL MATERIALS
DAY 1		
I. Welcome/Introduction to Seminar	lecture	transparencies
A.		
B.		
C.		
II. A.		
B.		
C.		
III. A.		
B.		
C.		
DAY 2		
I. A.		
B.		
C.		
II. A.		
B.		
C.		
III. A.		
B.		
C.		
IV. A. Wind-Up		
B.		

Ergonomics: Today and Tomorrow

You know that ergonomics is a powerful tool in helping organizations achieve such goals as increased productivity, cost containment, quality of products and services, and excellence. By using a macroergonomic or sociotechnical approach, management can integrate the various elements of ergonomics and set the stage for a smooth transition from the traditional office to an efficient, automated office.

PROJECT 1 ANSI STANDARDS

Objective: to answer questions regarding VDT standards.

Instructions

1. Read the monograph titled "The Ergonomic Perspective on Standards," (page 83) written by Dr. Gene Lynch, principal scientist in Human Factors Research at Tektronix Laboratories. Dr. Lynch chaired the Human Factors Society's VDT Standards Committee during the three years in which the technical content of ANSI/HFS-100 was developed.

2. Answer the questions on page 85.

PROJECT 2 THE IMPORTANCE OF ERGONOMICS IN THE OFFICE

Objective: to have students integrate their knowledge of ergonomics by completing the matrix and essay.

Instructions

1. You know that the Six Key Elements of ergonomics are job design, equipment, software design, workstation design, environment, and training. Note that the elements are listed across the top of the matrix shown on page 87. The eleven factors that affect the health, well-being, and performance of workers are listed down the left side of the matrix.

2. Using the matrix on page 87, rate those items on a 1–5 scale (5 being the highest) that "enter the picture" for each of the Key Ergonomic Elements listed. You will find some appropriate for many of the elements and some only applicable to one or two.

3. Then summarize your findings by writing an essay titled "The Importance of Ergonomics in Today's Office." Elaborate on two or three of the Six Key Elements that you think have the greatest impact upon the health, well-being, and performance of workers today.

PROJECT 3 ERGONOMICS AT WORK

Objective: to relate the knowledge of ergonomics acquired by students in this course to "real world" situations.

Instructions

1. Read the article titled "Ergonomics Isn't Last Year's Fad It's This Year's Profits" (pages 91 and 92). Note that several well-known experts in the field of ergonomics discuss their opinions on the connection between ergonomics and productivity.

2. After reading the article, identify the qualifications of each professional and explain in your own words his or her position on the issue he or she addresses in the article.

T. J. Springer (Qualifications)_____

_____

Position on issue_____

_____

Michael Brill (Qualifications)_____

_____

Position on issue_____

_____

Michael Smith (Qualifications)_____

_____

Position on issue_____

_____

Rani Lueder (Qualifications)_____

_____

Position on issue_____

_____

PROJECT 4 MANAGEMENT ACTION PLAN

Objective: to involve you in applying your knowledge of ergonomics as a means of making the transition from a manual to an automated system and thereby reduce resistance to change.

Instructions

1. Assume that you are a department manager at Social and Health Services of Boston. Top management is greatly concerned about the information which has been filtering to them through the office grapevine regarding the attitudes and fears the staff has toward the upcoming implementation of an automated system. Management purchased new chairs and adjustable furniture, but that has not seemed to allay the concerns about the overall impact the change will have. Management is trying to take an innovative, enlightened approach to the problem by developing a "key issue action plan" and asking for input from a task force consisting of a facilities manager, a department manager (you), the Human Resources director, a training administrator and one claims processor representative.

2. Using the sheet titled "Management Key Issue Action Plan" (page 89), address the issue presented by recommending three or four possible actions that could be taken to reach the objective. Include a proposed timetable (for example: weekly, ongoing, or a specific date) and identify a person (for example: yourself, Human Resources Manager, Department Manager) to be charged with following up to make sure the proposed actions are taken.

The Ergonomic Perspective

On Standards ·

Gene Lynch, Ph.D.

The American National Standard for Human Factors Engineering of Visual Display Terminal Workstations (ANSI/HFS-100) is now completed.

WHAT IS AN ANSI STANDARD?

ANSI is the American National Standards Institute. It is a clearing house for United States voluntary standards. All ANSI standards are voluntary. ANSI establishes procedures and processes for the writing and adoption of consensus standards. ANSI does not technically review or enforce standards.

HOW WAS ANSI/HFS-100 DEVELOPED?

The ANSI/HFS-100 was developed by a committee of the Human Factors Society accredited by ANSI to draft standards in the area of VDT use. The Human Factors Society is an interdisciplinary organization of over 4000 researchers and practitioners who design equipment, work, and environments to meet human strengths, capabilities and limitations. Seventeen Human Factors professionals from academia, industry, and government worked for three years developing, drafting and refining the standard. The result of this effort is the ninety page draft standard.

WHAT DOES THE STANDARD COVER?

The standard addresses the areas of physical and perceptual human factors (essentially ergonomics). The physical human factors include the environment, the physical design of the equipment and the furniture. The major perceptual human factors issue in visual display terminals is the quality of the displayed image. Issues which were specifically not included because they are not generally considered to be valid subjects for standardization, either due to a lack of reliable scientific data or because of current social practice, were software and work practices. These areas however are both recognized to be major contributors to worker productivity and job satisfaction and should be closely attended to by the manager.

WHAT IS THE PURPOSE OF THE STANDARD?

The purpose of the standard is to provide technical information on the "conditions that have been established as representing acceptable implementation of human factors engineering principles and practices in the design of visual display terminals (VDTs), associated furniture, and the work environ-ment in which they are placed." The standard was directed at the three most common applications; text processing, data entry and data inquiry.

WHO IS EXPECTED TO USE THIS STANDARD?

"As this is a technical standard, it is assumed that implementation of the standard will be by suitably trained and knowledgeable individuals. It is intended for use by professionals who have technical responsibility for the design, installation, and setup of VDTs, the associated furniture, and the work environments." For those with managerial responsibility, but not the technical expertise, the application of the standard to a particular site may require consultation with a human factors/ergonomics professional.

WHAT DOES CONFORMANCE TO THIS STANDARD MEAN?

Technically, conformance to the standard means that a complying system satisfies all the requirements found in the mandatory sections of the standard. These sections are indicated by the word "shall" in their statement. Sections with "should" in their statement are recommendations and are viewed as guidance. The spirit of the standard is to provide a satisfactory working environment for productivity and user comfort for the individual worker.

The standard is written from the perspective of the worker. The responsibility for compliance is a shared one. The manufacturer of the components of the work system needs to insure that they can be integrated into a complying system. The integrator must configure a complying system and the manager must select manufacturers and intergrators that provide a complying system. In the standard the manager is seen as an integrator of a system.

SIMPLY STATED, WHAT ARE THE LIGHTING REQUIREMENTS?

The illuminance shall not be so high as to wash out the image on the display. You have to be able to easily see the image and read information. The source of the illumination should not be seen as glare or disturbing reflections in the display. The actual lighting requirements for a particular office depend on the kind of work being done, need for paper documents, the print quality of these

The Joyce Institute

(continued)

documents, the kind of displays being used, and the characteristics of the user. The standard states that for most applications a minimum of 250 to 500 lux is sufficient and complying displays should be able to meet the image quality requirements at this level with no difficulty.

WHAT ARE THE NOISE LIMITS SPECIFIED IN THE STANDARD?

The standard recommends that the ambient sound pressure levels be less than 55 dBA and that impulsive noise and narrow band noise significantly above ambient should be avoided. This noise is measured from the operator's perspective and includes all the ambient noise including the equipment being operated.

The physical characteristics and arrangements of the environment have a great deal to do with the way sound is absorbed and reflected from surfaces. This makes it difficult to determine sound pressure levels (at the operator's ear) from the sound power levels which are measured and specified by equipment manufacturers.

WHAT DOES THE STANDARD SAY ABOUT HEATING AND VENTILATION ISSUES?

The standard references the ANSI/ASHRAE 55-1981 standard which describes the thermal parameters and comfort zones for work which is very similar to those covered by ANSI/HFS-100. In addition ANSI/HFS-100 requires that equipment be designed so that exhausting air is not directed toward the operator and that the equipment is arranged so that the exhausting air does not strike other workers. It requires that equipment be designed so that external surface tem-

peratures are less than 50° C.

It recommends that the heat build-up from the equipment under the worksurface be less than 3° C above the ambient temperature. This latter recommendation is a good example of the shared conformance issue. Both manufacture and integrator need to be aware of this recommendation.

DOES THE STANDARD TELL ME WHAT KIND OF COMPUTER EQUIPMENT TO BUY?

The standard does not specify kinds of equipment. The standard defines the characteristics for displays and keyboards which are important for effective and comfortable use of visual display terminals. These characteristics are in a combination of requirements and recommendations.

WILL I HAVE TO BUY NEW VDT FURNITURE?

No new furniture may be needed for individual situations. The furniture section of the standard was the most misunderstood section in the first review cycle. It has undergone extensive rewriting to clarify the intentions. The furniture section describes the characteristics of tables and chairs that are required and recommended for most configurations which will enhance work posture and comfort. The requirements and recommendations define those parameters and characteristics that should be considered in evaluating the suitability of a particular set of furniture for a particular individual. The standard should enable you to determine if an existing or proposed set of furniture is satisfactory for a given individual or a given range of individuals, working with a particular

set of equipment.

An existing desk, chair, computer terminal may be found to be satisfactory and in compliance with the standard for a particular individual and there would be no need for any modifications at all. The General Solution sections could also be used to prescribe changes to the existing furniture system that would bring it into compliance. Possibly the addition of a foot rest may be all that is needed.

IS THAT ALL THAT I NEED TO KNOW ABOUT THE STANDARD?

No. The standard is a ninety page technical document. What we have done here is simply address some relevant issues.

Dr. Lynch chaired the Human Factors Society's VDT Standards Committee during the three years in which the technical content of ANSI/HFS-100 was developed. Dr. Lynch is a principal scientist in Human Factors Research at Tektronix Laboratories. Tektronix is a manufacturer of engineering design, test, and measurement systems and a supplier of high quality graphics terminals and hard copy units to the scientific and engineering markets.

This monograph was written by Dr. Gene Lynch for use by The Joyce Institute for the purpose of disseminating information about the standards to its clients.

The Joyce Institute provides consulting services which enable clients to conform to the ANSI standards. The Joyce Institute, 1300 Plaza 600 Building, Seattle WA 98101, (206) 441-6745, 1-800-645-6045.

"THE ERGONOMIC PERSPECTIVE ON STANDARDS"

Indicate your answer to each of the following by circling "yes" or "no" in the answers column.

QUESTIONS	ANSWERS
1. ANSI reviews and enforces the standards it creates.	1. YES NO
2. ANSI stands for the American National Service Industry.	2. YES NO
3. The Human Factors Society is an interdisciplinary organization of researchers and practitioners who design equipment, work and environments to meet human strengths, capabilities, and limitations.	3. YES NO
4. The ANSI/HFS-100 addresses the areas of physical and perceptual human factors.	4. YES NO
5. The major perceptual human factors issue in visual display terminals is the quality of the displayed image.	5. YES NO
6. The standard also addresses software and work practices because of their importance relating to worker productivity and job satisfaction.	6. YES NO
7. The standard was directed at the three most common applications: text processing, data entry, and data inquiry.	7. YES NO
8. The standards are intended to provide guidelines for use by managerial and supervisory staff.	8. YES NO
9. "Shall" indicates mandatory standards and "Should" indicates recommended guidelines.	9. YES NO
10. The standard states that for most applications a minimum of 250 to 500 lux is sufficient lighting level.	10. YES NO
11. The standard recommends that the ambient sound pressure levels be less than 155 dB(A).	11. YES NO
12. The standard requires that equipment be designed so that external surface temperatures are less than 50°C.	12. YES NO
13. The standard specifies kinds of equipment which have the defined ergonomic characteristics.	13. YES NO
14. The standard recognizes that new chairs and furniture always be furnished.	14. YES NO
15. In the standard, the manager is seen as an integrator of a system.	15. YES NO

ERGONOMICS MATRIX

	SIX KEY ELEMENTS OF ERGONOMICS					
	Job Design	Equipment	Software Design	Work-station Design	Environment	Training
PLACES/THINGS Adjustability						
Comfort						
Safety						
Comprehensibility						
Reliability						
Usability						
TASKS Variety						
Identity/Importance						
Feedback						
Personal Growth						
Autonomy/Control						

MANAGEMENT KEY ISSUE ACTION PLAN

ISSUE: Staff seems apprehensive about the prospect of automation and their ability to adapt from the manual to the automated system for processing claims, billing clients, and communicating with various social and health services organizations.

OBJECTIVE: to maximize staff involvement in making the transition from the manual to the automated system and thereby reduce resistance to change.

ACTIONS TO BE TAKEN	TIMETABLE	PERSON RESPONSIBLE
1.		
2.		
3.		
4.		

The Automated Office

Ergonomics Isn't Last Year's Fad It's This Year's Profits

By the year 2000 we will be using processors that work at one billion instructions per second, with huge memories and screen resolution worthy of Hollywood movies. So says James Martin, automation futurist. Human futurists say we'll all be getting backaches at the terminal.

Ergonomists study healthy and unhealthy relationships between man and machines, such as the height at which a keyboard could begin to inflict lifelong pain on your wrist, or how often you'll have to take off work because the chair you're sitting in causes back pain. They're the ones predicting muscle problems, visual fatigue and general stress.

For managers it's a question of saving the company money as well as improving productivity in the department and keeping employees happy and healthy. T.J. Springer, ergonomist and president of Springer Associates, St. Charles, IL, says productivity improved 6% at a firm that repositioned and tilted terminals and replaced some glare-producing lights with fixtures that reduced glare. Employees could see the screen better. Springer is author of the book, *Improving Productivity In The Workplace, Reports From The Field,* which helps managers define and measure ergonomic problems and improvements. The book is available only through him. It is his contention that, in spite of the lack of perfect chairs, desks, lights and air systems, you can construct a beneficial work environment for employees, taking into account the particular tasks they perform.

Michael Brill, head of the Buffalo (NY) Organization for Social and Technological Innovation (BOSTI), has shown that if professional/technical employees perceive a drop in comfort of chairs and desks, productivity drops $701 per employee paid $31,600 a year. If this group lost privacy, it was worth $1,954. A $3,500 expenditure to move an employee from an open bullpen to a private area, with furniture improvements, returns $7,836 in productivity improvements in five years. Furniture payback is in 18 months.

So the argument that ergonomic furniture is not worth the expense doesn't hold water, in spite of the fact that healthy furniture does cost more than conventional chairs and desks.

Speakers at a recent Office Landscape Users Group (Philadelphia) conference in Chicago said the furniture industry is not putting enough research money into producing healthy furniture. Manufacturers have leapt ahead in the last three or four years, but they're not far enough along to have produced the furniture we need to automate in comfort, according to Michael Smith, former chief of occupational stress research at the National Institute for Occupational Safety and Health and professor at the University of Wisconsin, Madison.

FEAR IS A REAL PROBLEM

One of the gravest problems Smith has come across is that, in spite of the fact that studies show "there really is no increase in birth defects from VDT (radiation) exposure," no way has been found to allay continuing concern among computer operators over the problem.

Smith acknowledges that workers at VDTs suffer real visual discomfort. But this discomfort does not mean irreparable physical damage, he says. On the contrary, changing glare-producing lighting often corrects visual discomfort. Glare-reducing lights and screens can reduce typing errors. There are difficulties in settling on the best lighting, though. For instance, what is the best lighting for a worker with a VDT screen if the same worker looks at hard copy, which requires more light? This problem demands further study.

Smith was asked by one of the managers attending the conference whether the workplace *causes* problems or aggravates those that already exist in employees. The answer: The workplace causes them.

Rani Lueder agrees that furniture manufacturers just haven't devoted enough attention to the healthy workspace. She's a principal of Humanics, an ergonomics consulting firm in Encino, CA, and editor of *The Ergonomics Payoff,* Nichols Publishing Co., New York City, a book designed to introduce managers to all the issues involved in making the office healthy. Chapter titles include: "Stress in the Electronic Office," "Screen Visibility Requirements and Criteria," "Work Station Design," and "Space Planning."

The major office furniture manufacturers *were* paying a great deal of attention to ergonomic desks and chairs, although Europe is considered way ahead of the U.S. in design and use of health-producing office furniture. In fact, it was the Sensor chair, designed by Germany's Wolfgang Muller-Deisig, and brought out by Steelcase, Grand Rapids, MI, that received compliments from ergonomists. Knoll, New York City, also has focused attention on healthy chairs. More recently, however, ergonomics

By Megan Jill Paznik, Senior Editor

has seemingly fallen out of favor. I just don't hear about it as often as I used to. Is worker health passe? Have we gone far enough and now we'll stop? This just can't be allowed to happen if we're still looking forward to pain. Besides, even with the "good" furniture now available, how many companies have bought it for their employees—I mean for secretaries, not just for executives?

Lueder says 80% of all employees will have back problems stemming from inadequate support for the lumbar (lower back) region. Mind you, it's no easy task to design a proper chair for everyone. Women's hip sockets are forward of men's, probably to accommodate pregnancy, Lueder points out. That creates problems for appropriate chair design. Also, data entry

---

'Sheer demographics will promote better answers in the future. The population is aging, better educated and more affluent. There are more female workers, and they focus more on health issues than do men'

---

workers tend to lean forward when they type, which increases unhealthy curvature of the lower back, while other employees lean back. You'd either have to buy the correct chair for the job title, or get one flexible chair that accommodates both.

While these problems remain unsolved, Lueder says sheer demographics will promote better answers in the future. The population is aging, better educated and more affluent. There are more female workers, and they focus more on health issues than do men. By the time these workers are in their 40s they'll be experiencing back and vision problems, but they'll also be in high enough positions to do something about them. Let's hope so. If we do not get to work repairing our backs and eyes soon, we could be a damaged generation. Before we allow irreparable harm to our bodies, we should ask manufacturers what healthy offerings they have and insist on healthy answers. It might also be wise to consult with an ergonomics specialist, since, for a while, some manufacturers were calling everything they made "ergonomic."